The Academy of Golf at PGA National

Play Golf for Juniors

The Academy of Golf at PGA National

Play Golf for Juniors

Mike Adams
and T.J. Tomasi

FIREFLY BOOKS

A FIREFLY BOOK

Published by Firefly Books Ltd. 2000

First Printing

Canadian Cataloguing in Publication Data

Adams, Mike, 1954–
    Play golf for juniors

Includes index.
ISBN 1-55209-446-4

1. Golf for children – Juvenile literature. I. Tomasi, T.J. II. Title

GV966.3.A33.2000   j.796.352'083   C99-930936-6

Library of Congress Cataloguing in Publication Data

Adams, Mike, 1954–
    Play golf for juniors / Mike Adams and T.J. Tomasi.
[ ] p. : col. ill. ; cm.
At head of title : The Academy of Golf at PGA National.
Includes index.
Summary : Golf instruction for young people.
ISBN 1-55209-446-4
I. Golf – juvenile literature. [I. Golf.] I. Tomasi, T.J.
II. Academy of Golf at PGA National (Palm Beach, Fla.). III. Title.
796.352 -dc21   2000   CIP

Published in Canada in 2000 by
Firefly Books Ltd.
3680 Victoria Park Avenue
Willowdale, Ontario, M2H 3K1

Published in the United States in 2000 by
Firefly Books (U.S.) Inc.
P.O. Box 1338, Ellicott Station
Buffalo, New York 14205

Project coodinator: Steve Begandy
Project editor: Chris Hawkes
Project art director: Brian Flynn
Photographs: Justin Downing
Production: Bob Bhamra

Printed in Dubai

Contents

1 Introduction 6

2 Equipment 12

3 The Rules 22

4 On teaching your Junior 34

5 The Set-Up 44

6 Full Swing 58

7 The Short Game 86

8 Learning programs for juniors 118

Tournaments 126

Glossary 138

Index 142

Introduction

How important are you in the golf world as a junior golfer? Pretty important and your importance is on the rise. Junior golf is the fastest growing section of the golf market by far, so business wise dude, you're a player and they're going to pay attention to you. Another neat thing is that today, two out of every three high schools have a golf team so you've got a sport to play for your school. How many of you are they? Currently in the USA there are about five million juniors between ages of six and 18 playing golf on a regular basis and when you add in the rest of the world that number makes junior golf big.

What those statistics mean, as we shall see later in this book, is that as juniors, you have some buying power and business people are courting you with special programs, products and equipment. College golf has never been more popular and many of today's young athletes, like yourself, who used to focus on "big ball" games like baseball, football and basketball, are now choosing the "little ball" game of golf. Golf is a sport that is played in a drug-free atmosphere where, with the advent of the senior tour, the career is the same length as that of any business and easily the longest by far of any sport, except maybe fishing.

You even have yourself a magazine—that's very strong. It's called *Junior Golf Magazine* and here's their message to you in a nutshell: "You [the junior player] have the access to play, the equipment to use, the instructions to learn by, but the final impression is yours to make. Know the rules, know the etiquette and respect the game. You have the opportunity your parents did not have. Seize the moment and have fun. It is a special time for junior golf." And, of course, this is exactly why we wrote this book.

So welcome to golf. You're about to begin a real adventure into a lifetime of fun. Hitting a perfect shot like a long, solid drive that carries the fairway bunker and lands in a perfect position, or a well-placed iron that finishes close to the pin—what a trip. You'll hit some shots as well as any pro who ever lived and you'll hit a bunch of clunkers too. But here's

The authors—Mike Adams (left) and T.J. Tomasi.

the thing about golf that you've got to love—it's you and only you. There is no team so there's no one to blame if you screw up, but you get all the credit if you do something great. Everyone owes a big thank you to the Scots, an independent bunch, who invented the game in the 17th century.

By its very nature, golf appeals to independent people; you get what you hit, everybody has the same chance to do well and they're governed by a set of rules that apply to everyone. At the end of the game you just count up and see who won—no judges who like one kid better than the other; no bias rules that apply to some but not to all. In golf it's blame or fame; its all you and that makes golf both fair and fascinating. Think of it this way: in sports where you play against somebody, your actions are partly a response to their performance and what they do dramatically affects what you do. For example, a pitcher's choice of a curve ball versus a fast pitch determines what you do as the batter and the server in tennis dictates the response of the opponent on the other side of the net. But in golf, you start and finish everything because, by the rules of the game, the ball doesn't move unless you act on it. What you do to that ball depends solely on your own capabilities, laced with a little luck.

And did we mention that you can play it all your life? We did but here's more. That might not mean much to you now, but ask your dad or your mom, they'll tell you. Most of the golfers on the PGA Senior Tour say they're playing better golf now than they played on the regular tour. Gymnasts are "old" at 30 years of age and baseball players don't play much past 40, but at 60, you can just be hitting your stride in golf. We know 60 seems like a lifetime away—come to think of it, maybe that's why they call golf "the game for a lifetime".

Another good thing about golf is that to play it well, you don't have run fast, throw a ball a long way or be strong enough to lift heavy weights—bigger isn't better and neither is smaller—basically it doesn't matter. A golfer with a good short game is a match for any one even if she or he doesn't drive it a mile. It is part of the fascination and frustration of the game that a three-foot putt and a 300-yard drive are of equal value on your scorecard. Tiny Paul Runyan beat the mighty "Slammin Sammy" Snead head to head for the PGA championship some 40 years ago, even though Runyan was consistently out-driven, sometimes by as much as 100 yards. And while you're much too young to have been born, the dominant golfers in the 1960s and 1970s were called the "Big Three", but one of them, Gary Player, was only 5ft 6ins and 145 pounds and he more than held his own.

And it's the same today; in golf David versus Goliath is even money. So even though today's athletes are much bigger and stronger than in the past, golf remains one of the few sports where big versus small carries no weight; both Corey Pavin and Ernie Els are world-class players as are Laura Davies and Patty Sheehan. One way of looking at it is that golf is truly democratic, as long as you satisfy the laws of physics, anyone can play and play well—and that includes you.

Here's what's in the book:

Chapter 1
Equipment

Is it the archer or the arrows? Well it's both and this chapter is about your clubs, you know, the things you hit the ball with. In the last ten years, the use of the computer documents that the effects of club specifications,

The game of golf is a game for life—and it's fun!

such as loft and lie, on the flight of the golf ball are substantial. The results of the research are clear: learning to swing the golf club correctly is directly dependent on having the correct golf club to swing. To maximize your performance in golf, you should fit your golf clubs to your own personal characteristics—such as swing speed, strength, and your body size.

What are the important specifications you need in your equipment to make sure you can make a good swing? Now there's often a big difference between what you need and what you want (remember the line from the Rolling Stones song "You can't always have what you want") and in this chapter we'll just focus on what you need.

Chapter 2
The Rules

You can go out and just hit the ball around, but if you want to play the game called golf there are rules and in this chapter we review the only ones you really have to know. Playing by the rules lets you know how good you really are and it's fun because you're playing the same exact game as the pros are—at least rules wise.

Big or small, boy or girl, golf is a truly democratic game.

And how about a word on how to behave (this isn't for you because you're a perfect kid, it's for all the other kids reading this). Golf has a rich history as played by gentle men and women and this section on etiquette suggests a few basic dos and don'ts that every golfer should know and observe.

Chapter 3
How To Teach Your Kid Golf

This chapter, mom and dad, is for you. We know you're interested in helping your kid to play better golf so we included non-technical information on how kids learn that will help you teach your junior. But remember, you're a guide not a jailer.

Chapter 4
Full Swing

So you think you're doing it right, well here's a chance to match yourself up with the kids in the book. You never can tell, maybe you're better than they are so next time you'll be in the book with other kids copying you. We'll start with the grip and cover the entire stance and swing. Our models are good players, who are 11, 13, 15, 17 years old respectively.

Chapter 5
The Short Game

Since approximately 65 per cent of the strokes you take are from 100 yards and in, pitching, putting, chipping and sand play make up an important segment of your blueprint for better golf. Even the best pros in the world miss on average about six greens a round, yet they manage to shoot par or better. Obviously then, how you handle the close shots from just off the green, plays a major role in how well you score or, if you don't care about score, how well you're playing your game.

Chapter 6
Group Learning

Group Learning is an important part of learning golf for kids and we'll outline what kind of programs are out there for you to take advantage of and how a good junior golf program is structured.

Chapter 7
Tournaments

So you're ready to play in tournaments? Here's what you should know, including how to play tournament golf (on course strategy) and where the competition is on a national level.

As you can see from this brief overview, the purpose of this book is quite simply to help you play better golf. In the final analysis, your development depends on your ability to learn—our job is to get you started in the right direction.

So let's get to it!

1 Equipment

It doesn't matter if you're a beginner or an old pro (well maybe a new pro at your age), it's important that your clubs fit you. Here's a piece of advice, "don't use hand-me-down clubs that were built for adults." Your dad's shoes probably don't fit you and neither do his clubs, matter of fact they might not even fit him. Misfits hurt both your feet and your golf game. Hand-me-downs may be free, but they'll cost you, because if you're playing with cut-down adult clubs, the chances are the shafts are way too stiff, and they're too heavy with lie angles that are too upright.

We'll explain all this below, but basically do anything you can to get clubs to fit you—go on a hunger strike, throw a tantrum or refuse to watch television (this irrational act will scare them) until you get your clubs. Better still, show the management (dad and mom) a picture of a palatial house and mention that Tiger Woods bought his parents a home like this, with his first $40 million pay check. They'll get the point and you'll get the clubs.

It is important to get the right weight of club for the perfect swing (2). If the club is too heavy for you, there is a danger that you'll overswing (1).

So which clubs should you have? In this chapter you'll learn how the individual specifications of a golf club affect your ability to swing the club and therefore how your ball responds. We'll limit our look to six important features that influence performance: shaft flex, weight, length, lie angle, loft and grip size. It is our opinion that while you probably don't need the most expensive set on the market, you do need to be custom fit by an expert fitter. The idea that you don't need a good set while you're learning the game is a dangerous one. In fact, a misfit set of clubs during the learning stage will force you into so many bad habits and ruinous swing compensations, that your swing may never recover. Yes, we know that Seve Ballesteros learned to play with a set of one—one club that is, a three iron. But you don't think it would have ruined him if he'd started with a perfectly fit set of clubs do you?

Six Important Club Specifications

Club Weight

The correct overall weight as well as the right clubhead weight is a very important club specification. As a young player your muscles haven't filled in yet and if the club is too heavy you'll "over swing", that is where you lose control of the club allowing the club shaft to drop way past the proper parallel position at the top of your swing.

There are really two "types" of weight and they're very different. Swing weight is the relation of the length of the club to the weight in the

Clubhead Speed

How fast you swing your club, while not the only factor, is a starting point for finding the right shaft for your clubs.

(There is a special device that measures your club head speed in miles per hour just a few inches before you make contact with the ball).

A rule of thumb is if you swing under 60 mph, you'd use a very flexible shaft. These shafts are usually marked with an "F" for flexible.

With a speed between 60 to 80 mph, a slightly less flexible "A" shaft may work best. It's commonly known as a men's "senior shaft" or a strong "junior shaft", but here again gender and age are really irrelevant because the shaft doesn't know how old you are and physics doesn't care.

An "R" or regular shaft is the next step, and is suggested for those who swing from 81 to 94 mph.

These shafts were generally the standard for very strong female juniors and strong, male juniors.

An "S" on the shaft stands for stiff and "XS" for extra stiff. These are the least flexible shafts and a high swing speed is required to make them flex and kick into the ball correctly. Very strong male juniors who are ready for college golf are often in this category.

clubhead. It's measured in ounce/inches and terms you often hear like C7, or D4, are related to how much you'll feel the clubhead while it's in motion. "Static weight", or "dead weight" as it's sometimes called, is the actual weight of the club measured in ounces. Just as you weigh 90 pounds (or whatever), your club's static weight might be 12 ounces. You want to swing the club rather than let the club swing you, so we recommend the lightest static weight that feels good to you and that will allow you to "own the club" while you swing it. In other words you need to have control of the club and unless you're big and strong, as a junior, adult clubs are just too heavy.

Shaft Flex

For the most part you have to watch out for club shafts that are too stiff for you. It's much better to swing a shaft that's too whippy because, after you hit enough balls, the only way you can hit decent shots with a whippy shaft, is to slow down. There's even a teaching aid on the market that we use with a shaft so flexible you have to be ultra smooth. It's a great aid, but you wouldn't want to play with it so the best deal is to have a shaft whose flex is just right for you.

We often use this analogy to show the importance of the shaft: you can think of the shaft as "the engine of the club", and if the shafts in your clubs are wrong for you, they're no more useful to you than a car without an engine. When your shafts are too stiff you can't square the clubhead to the ball at impact and, because stiff shafts make it hard to get the ball in the air unless they fit you, you'll hang on your back foot to get the ball airborne. Just the opposite happens when your shafts are too flexible—the tendency is to lunge at the ball and try to keep the clubface from snapping shut. So if you want a powerful kick to your shots, a square clubface at impact and a well-balanced swing, make sure you get the right shaft flex in your clubs.

What about Graphite?

Graphite and other lightweight materials such as titanium have made it possible to move more weight into the clubhead for higher, more powerful shots. The problem is they are expensive and since you're growing fast and will need to replace your clubs several times before you get to adulthood, steel shafts are your best bet. But if the Management

Notice the difference between a set up where the shaft is too long (1) leaving the player off balance and the correct shaft length (2).

will foot the bill, go for the graphite shafts and throw in a titanium clubhead—and why not a new wardrobe while you're at it.

Shaft Length

Here is a good phrase to remember—"too long is wrong"—but that's what often happens when juniors are misfit, i.e. the clubs are usually too long. Here is why the wrong length is no good. How you stand to the ball (your golf posture) and your balance while you swing, are related. If your clubs aren't the right length, you'll be forced into an unbalanced position before you even swing. If you start out-of-balance at address you'll struggle for your balance throughout your swing and since you don't want to fall on your face, you're much more interested in keeping your balance than hitting the ball. Generally if your clubs are too long, your swing will be on the flat side because you must stand too far away from the ball. You'll swing too much around your body and hit shots that are too low. Conversely if you're clubs are too short, you'll stand over the ball in a crowded hunch that encourages an upright plane, and you just lift the club abruptly to the top of your swing then chop down on the ball—ouch.

In addition to creating posture and balance problems, clubs that are the

The Big Dog

TIPS

What about the big stick, the long bomber, the Big Dog? Is longer better? Does a longer shaft in your driver mean a longer drive? Not always. Your driver is designed to hit the ball longer than any of your other clubs and to maximize your distance off the tee, you need the right length. It's like anything else, you can overdo a good thing by making your shaft too long. How can you tell? Use clubface tape and hit 20 balls on two different days with drivers of different lengths. The one with the most center hits is the one for you.

wrong length disrupt your ability to hit the sweet spot of your clubface consistently. If your clubs are too short and you make a good swing, you'll make contact with the ball on the toe. If your clubs are too long, you'll hit near the heel. Studies show that for every $1/2$ inch you hit off the center of an iron you lose approximately five per cent in total distance and with woods it's about seven per cent, so you can't just add length to your clubs and expect to get more distance.

As we have said, the only way you can be sure that the length of a set of clubs is right for you is to test them dynamically—hit with them. Your golf professional can apply a special tape to the face of the club so that when you hit the ball it leaves a mark on the face. After 10 or 15 balls a clear pattern should develop, ideally in the center of the clubface.

Grip Size

Your hat has to fit your head, your pants fit your waist and your golf club grip should fit the size of your hand. Here's how you can measure to see if it does: when you're gripping the club properly, the tip of your left-hand ring finger should just barely touch the heel pad of your left hand (*see chapter four on set up*). If there's a gap, your grips are too big and if one or more of your fingers is digging into your heel pad your grips are too small.

Big Hands-Big Hook

You may not think so, but grip size and how far you hit the ball are related. How? Because you need the right grip pressure to make a powerful release of your wrists and arms and oversized grips force you to hold the club too much in the palms of the hands. This translates into restricted wrist action and a short slice. On the other hand, play with too small a grip and you'll overuse your hands giving your swing that flippy look and worse, your ball that hooky look.

What your grip is made of obviously affects the feel, and the type of grip you want is simply a personal preference. Some players like a smooth, leathery feel while others like the rougher feel of a cord grip. A word of caution though. If you play golf in hot, humid conditions, the cord is less likely to slip in your hands. Keep your grips clean by washing them with warm soapy water, then rinse and dry them. And change them when they get slippery or they'll be too difficult to control.

TIPS *Avoid the trap that most adults fall into: the markings on the grip are not guides of where you should place your hands so when you take your grip on the club be sure to ignore the markings on the grip.*

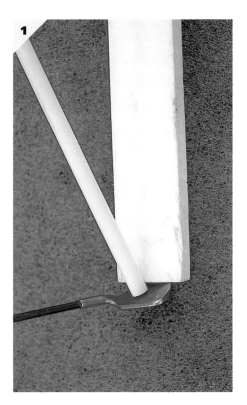 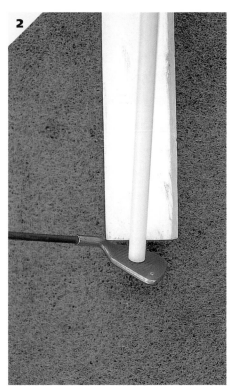 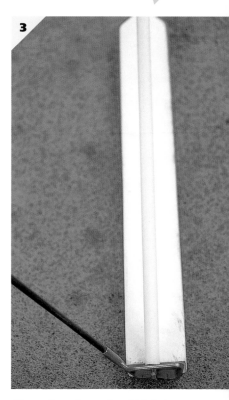

Lie angle: a lie angle which is too far off the ground will cause the shot to go left (1); too far towards the ground and the shot will go right (2). (3) shows the perfect lie angle.

Lie Angle

The lie angle is measured by a line from the center line of the shaft to the ground when the club is soled correctly. When it's correct, the bottom of the club is flush to the ground (except the toe is in the air a bit), the face aims straight ahead, and the loft is correct. For this to happen, your clubs must have the correct lie angle, a specification that varies depending on the individual.

Here's something not many adults know and you should point this out if they try to give you their old clubs: all clubs are built with the toe slightly in the air to account for the bowing of the shaft toward the ground when you swing. The angle that the shaft is drilled into the neck of the club is called the lie and you should have your lies checked because some lies are good and some are bad.

Here's the scoop on why lie angles are important: a lie angle with the toe of the club too far off the ground at impact causes your ball to go to the left of target even if you made a perfect swing. If the toe of your clubhead is too far toward the ground, your ball goes to the right of the target. It could be your swing or it could be your clubs (or it could be both), but the point is have them checked [the clubs], because with the wrong lie angle you have to make a bad swing to hit a good shot and that's no way to develop a good golf swing. How can you have them checked? Most golf professionals have access to a machine that adjusts clubs to the proper lie angle by bending the shaft near the neck of your club. To test the lie, they will put a piece of tape on the sole of your club and have you hit balls off what's known as a lie board. If the lie angle is correct for you, the tape will show one kind of mark; if the lie is incorrect the tape will show another kind of mark.

Divots Can Tell You A Lot

You can get some information on your lie angles by checking out your divots. If they're deeper on the outside of the divot, it's caused by the toe digging into the ground and it may be your lie is too flat. If they're deeper near the heel, or they're pie shaped, your clubs are too upright. Pie-shaped divots that narrow to a point after the ball are often an indication that the heel hit the ground first and flipped the toe shut. Now one or two bad divots don't tell the story, but when you see a pattern that continually re-occurs, then it's time to go to a club-fitting expert.

Loft

Loft is how much your clubface looks at the sky when it sits correctly behind the ball and it has a major affect on the height of your golf shot. Loft is measured in degrees, so the face of your sandwedge would look at the sky a lot (say 56 degrees) and your driver might have only 13 degrees, which means that the sandwedge hits very high, short shots and the driver hits much lower and longer shots. This is why you'd mostly use the driver or three wood off the tee and the sandwedge near the green. Guess the club with the lowest loft in your bag? You are correct once again—it's the putter, but even that has a couple of degrees, sometimes as many as five.

Why One Iron Goes Farther Than Another

Usually there are four degrees of loft difference between each of your irons, for example, your pitching wedge might have 48 degrees of loft and your nine iron, 44 degrees, your eight iron, 40 degrees, and so on. For each degree of loft on a well struck shot, you can count on the ball flying $2^1/_2$ yards, so with four degrees between each club, that's about ten yards

Notice the difference in loft between the two clubs.

of difference between each iron. Obviously it's essential to know how far you hit each club. It doesn't help much to know it's 155 yards to the flag if you don't know which club moves your ball 155 yards.

Start With Your Eight

First find out how far you hit your average eight iron. Go to the range and hit a bunch of balls and watch how far they fly—on average let's say it's 110 yards. Since you know that you have ten yards between each club that means your seven iron should go 120 yards and your nine iron, 100 yards. Now when you're on the course and it's 130 yards to the flag, what club would you choose? Six iron is correct.

   Note that if you are a young junior or not very strong, your longer irons probably all go about the same distance because of your low swing speed. Here is where you should use the seven and nine woods described below, instead of the longer irons.

A Beginner's Set

TIPS

When you're just starting out in golf it's not necessary to have a full set of clubs and it may be best to have only five. A putter, sandwedge, seven iron, seven wood and three wood will get you started and give you an idea of the different length and height each club is supposed to travel.

Utility Woods

For all but the low handicap older junior, we firmly recommend utility woods, like the seven, nine and even the 11, in place of your long irons. Utility woods are easier to hit from different lies and because they have a bigger sweet spot, you'll see a difference in how far you hit the ball. Utility woods have wide soles that are specially designed to make the club skim over a tight lie where the ball sits down and you can't get at it with a long iron. Also, they're designed so they won't get caught in high grass as much as an iron will. There are some players on the PGA Tour and the Senior Tour that have a seven wood in the bag and Annika Sorenstam, the 1995 and 1996 US Open Champion, carries a seven and sometimes a nine wood while Liselotte Neumann, winner of the 1988 US Open, carries a nine and an 11 wood (and no irons longer than a six), so don't be shy about using them.

Putters

Choosing a putter is a matter of feel and confidence and there aren't any rules for how you select one. Some pros change their putter often, depending on how it's currently working. It is said that Arnold Palmer has over 1,000 putters in his garage all of which he has tried throughout his long career, whereas Ben Crenshaw has stayed faithful to his old blade putter. And somewhere in-between is probably you.

Putters are made in three basic styles: the box, the blade and the mallet. The box putter, because they put the weight around the edges, gives you a bigger sweet spot and, therefore, more margin for error if you hit slightly off center. Blade putters have the majority of weight in the center of the clubface and are often the choice of good putters with very consistent putting strokes. Mis-hits are more likely to roll off line, but centered hits stay straight and true. The mallet putter usually has a heavy head. If you're a handsy putter whose left wrist breaks down through impact, the weight of the mallet could help you make more of a "stroking" motion. Therefore, you should definitely try a heavy headed putter on slow greens, because the extra weight gives you a firmer roll without getting wristy.

Wedges

The performance of your wedge is related to how the sole (the bottom of the club) is built. Bounce, how much the bottom of your wedge sticks out, is what makes the club good at bouncing off the ground rather than digging into it. The greater the bounce, the farther the sole extends below the leading edge, the less likely the clubhead will dig into the ground.

Wedge comes in a variety of lofts. Many players, including experts, carry three wedges in their bag, pitching, sand and lob wedge. Some even carry a fourth called a gap wedge which you don't have to worry about right now. A pitching wedge with 50 degrees of loft and about four degrees of bounce, works well from tight lies and from the fairway. The average sandwedge has around 56 degrees loft with 11 degrees of bounce to prevent the leading edge from digging into the sand. It works well in soft sand and around the greens in normal green-side rough. As Chi Chi Rodriguez says: "I'll never go hungry playing golf, 'cos I always have my sand-which." A bad joke to tell, but a good club to carry.

Notice the "bounce" on the wedges pictured above.

Your sandwedge has the most loft of all the clubs in your regular line-up, so your shots fly high and land softly, a necessity in those situations when you don't have much putting green to work with. The lob wedge, a special club not included in the standard set, which is even more lofted than your sandwedge, should stay out of your bag. Why? Because leaving it out will develop your touch by forcing you to learn to hit all the types of shots around the green with your sandwedge. Remember that in the last analysis, it's touch that allows you to handle those tough greenside shots over bunkers or water, from lies you rarely practice from. We mentioned earlier in this chapter that Seve Ballesteros had only had one club to play with as a kid—a three iron. Instead of a hindrance, he said it was the reason he was so good around the greens as a pro—by playing with only one club he learned touch. Later on you can add a lob wedge if you must, but for now the lob is out of a job.

The Rules

You can go out and just hit the ball around, but if you want to play the game called golf there are rules and in this chapter we review the only ones you really have to know. Playing by the rules lets you know how good you really are and it's fun because you're playing the same exact game as the pros are—at least rules wise.

And how about a word on how to behave (this isn't for you because you're a perfect kid, it's for all the other kids reading this). Golf has a rich history as played by gentle men and women and this section on etiquette suggests a few basic dos and don'ts that every golfer should know and observe.

For Brand New Golfers Only

What's Par

Let's start at the very beginning with the concept of par. You may have heard the phrase, "it's par for the course." Well it comes from the number of times it takes an expert to hit the ball from the teeing ground into the hole. A normal golf course has 18 different holes consisting of a mixture of par threes, par fours and par fives. On par threes, the shortest holes, the expert playing his or her best game is expected to hit the ball from the tee to the green in one shot. On par fours, the intermediate distance holes, the tee shot lands in the fairway and from there the "approach shot" lands on the green. On par fives, the longest holes on the course, it takes three shots to reach the green. Once you reach each green you're allotted two putts to make your score equal to par.

These examples are what's know as a "regulation par", but since golf is a game where mis-hits are common, even the world's best players sometimes struggle to make par in "regulation", which is why having a good short game is so important. Even the best pros in the world miss on average about six greens and a couple of fairways per round, yet they manage to shoot par or better, so read the short game section very carefully.

The par for each hole is written on the scorecard. Most scores for the average junior golfer will be more than par or "over par" and on rare occasions you'll put your ball in the hole in fewer strokes than par and you'll be "under par". When you take one stroke more than par, you've made what's known as a bogey; two strokes more than par is a double bogey. Guess what a triple and quadruple bogey are (right—three and four over par). If you take one stroke less than par, you've made a birdie (that's good), two strokes less is an eagle (terrific), three less is a double eagle (call your agent). If your tee shot goes straight into the hole that's known as a hole-in-one, and the soft drinks are on you. So now that you know all about par, it's time to go to the course.

Off to the Course

It's fun to practice, but as soon as you get your swing in reasonable shape it's time to play golf on the course. Our suggestion is that you just have fun out there, but also that you be a "good citizen" on the course, so you don't make it tough for the other golfers by not knowing what to do. The golf course is a community of folks, some old, some young, some beginners and some expert; it's the kind of mix where you can find about any type of person and like anywhere you go (the movies, school, Wally World), the mix demands that there are guidelines to follow. For this reason, we suggest some changes in the rules you can make as a new golfer that will allow you to keep up with the pace of play on the course. So here are some special "rules" for playing golf that are not really rules at all—just common sense. Please keep in mind that our suggestions are not in accordance with the official *Rules of Golf*, and are by no means suggested for play other than as outlined here.

Rule 1: No Mulligans

You see it all the time; a group of adults tee off and they all take second and sometimes third shots until they got one they like. And you can bet they are just the ones who complain about slow play. Taking a "mulligan" (golf lingo for another try), is a common practice, but regardless of what the adults do, don't you do it. Mulligans take too long and if you're a beginner, it's likely you'll hit the same or an even worse shot again and then you'll be looking for two balls instead of one. It's important to remember the other members of your group are eager for their own turn to play, and hitting a second ball from the same place means they must wait while you hit another ball. And the superintendent won't appreciate the extra divots you might make either. Now we advocate bending the rules for a while, to make the game easier and faster, but the essence of golf is that you're forced to play your mistakes. Mulligans are contrary to the nature of the game and not a good habit to start.

Rule 2: Don't Dawdle

In golf you can get your ball into places it will take all day to get out of, or at least it seems like all day to the people behind you. And since you're not keeping score anyway, don't be shy about picking your ball up. For

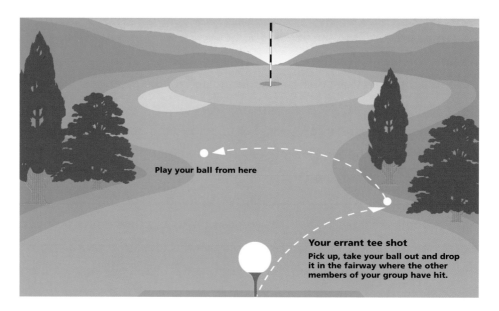

Play your ball from here

Your errant tee shot
Pick up, take your ball out and drop it in the fairway where the other members of your group have hit.

example, if you hit a ball that goes only a few yards off the tee, pick it up and bring it forward to the fairway where you can play it. During your first few rounds you may find that several shots in a row go very badly. No big deal. Instead of frustrating yourself and worrying about holding up the other members of your group just pick up your ball, and take another turn after the others have hit.

Rule 3: "Eight is Enough"

A very simple suggestion that will make you fun to play with—if there are golfers behind you who are playing faster, let them play through. If the course is crowded so it does no good to let just one group through, pick your ball up after eight swings and go to the next tee. As you get better you'll find you don't use this rule as much, in fact why not keep track of how many pick-ups you have and watch with pride as the number drops like a stone as you improve. And speaking of improving, how about your lie (how the balls sits on the ground), can you improve that?

Rule 4: Improving Your Lie

Especially during your first few rounds move your ball from difficult lies (heavy rough, bare ground, difficult stance) onto good ones. If someone tells you you're breaking the rules, explain to them that you're trying to learn the easier shots before you tackle the more difficult ones and you're not playing for an official score. There is little sense in trying to hit a ball from heavy rough when, like most new golfers, you're still challenged by a shot from a good lie in the fairway. We recommend that you use a tee on all shots the first few times you play. Why not, it will make it more fun.

To start with, move your ball from an unplayable lie to a better one—it's more important to learn the easier shots as a beginner.

Rule 5: Putt Limit

There is nothing that takes more time or is more annoying to the people waiting to hit than a golfer taking five putts or more. So make it a rule: If you've already taken three, do yourself and your companions a favor and pick the ball up. The rule: limit putts to three.

Rule 6: Be Ready

Always be ready to play when it's your turn. Get to your ball, plan your shot, select the club and when it's safe—fire.

Rule 7: Watch Your Ball

One thing you can't forget to do is watch your ball after you hit it. Too many juniors turn away when they hit a bad shot and lose track of the ball. So make sure you follow the ball to its final destination with your eyes. And don't rely on others to tell you where it is—half the time they're not watching and the rest of the time they don't really care, so it's up to you. Oh and don't be like the others—watch the ball when someone else is hitting so you can tell them where it went.

Rule 8: A Once-Around for a Lost Ball

By strict rule a player has five minutes to find his ball, but here's our rule: take one quick look around the general area and if you can't find it, play your shot from that area. If you spent five minutes looking for each ball and you lost six balls that's 30 minutes just looking. So don't do a search— do a once-around.

Playing Real Golf

So now you're a lot better than you were a few paragraphs ago and it's time for real, by-the-rules golf. As we said in the introduction, you can go out and just hit the ball around, but if you want to play the game called golf there are a set of rules by which to play and in this chapter we review the only ones you have to know to get started. Playing by the rules lets you know how good you really are and once you've got a decent swing it's fun, because you're playing the same game as the pros are (well, rule-wise anyway).

A Few Rules You Should Know

Since it's important to learn and play by the rules as soon as you're ready, you'll find a simple description below of some rules you'll deal with most frequently. Please keep in mind, however, that the official rules are far more complex and the following is only a generalized description of a few rules to get you off to a good start.

The Last Shall Be First

Who plays first off the first tee is determined by lot—flip a coin or toss a tee and who it points to when it lands, is up. Thereafter the order is determined by honors: the golfer with the lowest score hits first, the next lowest second and so on. If everyone makes the same score, the order from the previous tee applies so the last golfer to play first, plays first again.

Who's Away?

After teeing off, if you're farthest from the hole, you hit first.

Play the ball as it lies—even if it's out of a divot.

Golf's Basic Rule

Once you hit your ball from the teeing ground it's in play and you can't do anything that improves the lie of your ball or your swing, such as breaking or ripping up anything fixed or growing. If you're playing "real" golf, follow the basic rule of golf, which is play your ball as you find it and only move it by hitting it with your club or in accordance with the rules. This is called "playing it as it lies". This means, once you start to play for an official score, the rules prevent you from moving your ball except under certain conditions, one of which is on the putting green. Once you're on the putting green, the rules allow you to lift and clean your ball after you've marked its location with a coin or similar object. To be on the safe side, don't touch the line of your putt on the green except to fix a ball mark or to remove loose impediments like a leaf or anything man made.

Now there are times, when you don't have to swing at the ball to improve your position. Let's say your ball is stuck in a bramble bush or a deep rut made by a maintenance vehicle. There's no way you can hit your ball out of either situation, so by rule, you can take what's called a drop.

The Power of Tiger Woods

TIPS

Now we all know how far Tiger hits the ball, but at the 1999 Phoenix Open he showed another power—the power to move 1,000lb rocks. It happened like this. Tiger blew his tee shot so far off the tee on one hole that it went through the fairway and stopped six inches from a big rock. Even though it was a long par five, he could reach the green with an iron from where he was, if it weren't for that rock blocking his path. Now Tiger is not only young, rich, and the world's best golfer, he's also very smart and he knows about something called a "loose impediment" which is defined as "natural objects such as stones ... not fixed or growing ... or solidly embedded". Tiger called a rules official and claimed the rock was a loose impediment because it wasn't fixed, growing or embedded. The official agreed, so Tiger gave the nod to some beefy fans and they moved the rock out of the way and Tiger went on to make a birdie. So remember if it's a loose impediment, you (or your friends) can move it.

Two Kinds of Drops

Now there are two kinds of drops: a free drop and a penalty drop. If you take a drop and it costs you a stroke penalty under the rules (like for an unplayable lie) you're always entitled to two club lengths relief. But it's

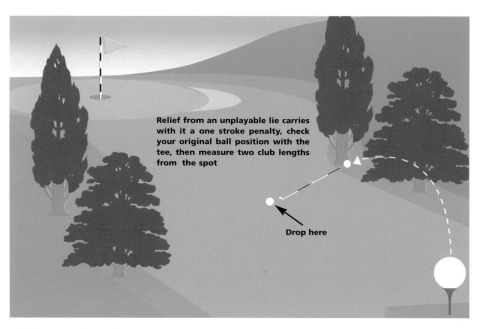

Relief from an unplayable lie carries with it a one stroke penalty, check your original ball position with the tee, then measure two club lengths from the spot

Drop here

different when the drop is "free"—say you're in ground under repair—then you get only one club length.

Before you lift your ball for a drop, always mark its position with a tee and leave the tee in the ground until after you've hit the shot, so if

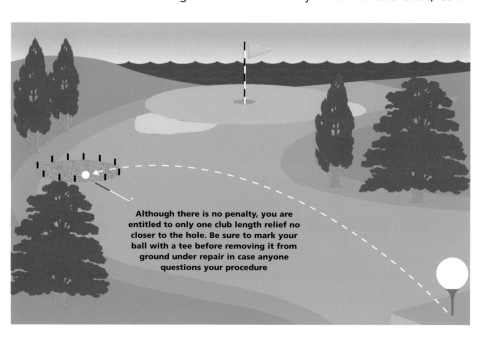

Although there is no penalty, you are entitled to only one club length relief no closer to the hole. Be sure to mark your ball with a tee before removing it from ground under repair in case anyone questions your procedure

someone questions your procedure, you can prove exactly what you did. At no time can you drop or place your ball closer to the hole.

Is This My Ball?

Knowing a ball is your ball is not as easy as it sounds. Now it's easy to identify your ball when you are carrying it in your hand or when you have positioned it on the tee box, but remember that after you hit it, your ball (hopefully) will be far away, so how do you know that it's your ball after it leaves the tee? The answer is simple; do like the pros do and mark your ball with a magic marker using some cool sign like your name, a couple of dots or a sentence like, "What are you doing just lying there?"—it doesn't matter just as long as you can identify it. And check it before each stroke to make sure it's your ball because there's a penalty for playing the wrong ball.

Make sure you know the ruling on loose impediments.

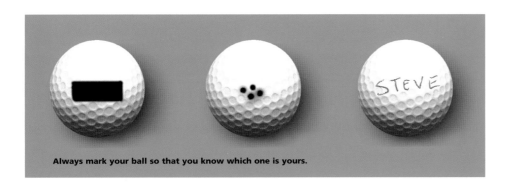

Always mark your ball so that you know which one is yours.

Hazards

When your ball lands in a bunker, one of golf's two official hazards, you're not allowed to let your club touch the sand until you actually make your downswing, so be sure to hover your club above the sand when you take your address position. As we saw in the Tiger Woods incident, you're allowed to remove "loose impediments", such as stones, fallen branches and leaves, except inside the boundaries of a hazard, where you can only remove man-made things such as paper cups, bottles or cigarette stubs. If your ball rolls just inside the boundary of a water hazard, which is marked by yellow (regular) or red (lateral) stakes, you're allowed to play your ball if you can, but remember, as in the bunker, you can't "ground" your club at address in this hazard either.

Most often though, when you hit it in a water hazard, you won't be able to play it. The procedure is to add a one stroke penalty to your score and drop your ball according to the rules. To do so, you'll need to figure out which type of water hazard you're in. A regular water hazard is defined by yellow stakes and lies between the fairway and the hole.

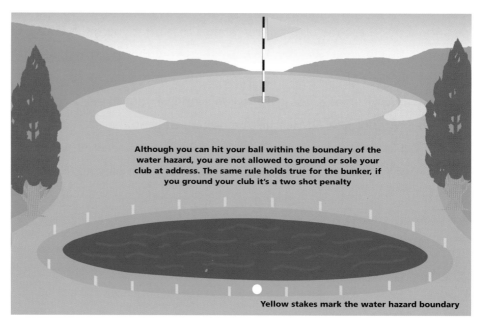

Although you can hit your ball within the boundary of the water hazard, you are not allowed to ground or sole your club at address. The same rule holds true for the bunker, if you ground your club it's a two shot penalty

Yellow stakes mark the water hazard boundary

You can drop your ball any distance behind the hazard on a line with the hole and the point where your ball last crossed the hazard line. A lateral water hazard is marked by red stakes and runs alongside the fairway and

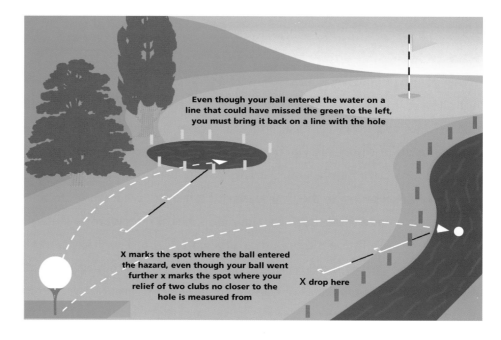

Even though your ball entered the water on a line that could have missed the green to the left, you must bring it back on a line with the hole

X marks the spot where the ball entered the hazard, even though your ball went further x marks the spot where your relief of two clubs no closer to the hole is measured from

X drop here

the green. In most cases, if you follow the fairway, you don't have to play over a lateral hazard as you do when confronted with a regular water hazard. Though the rules allow several options for a lateral hazard, the most common is to drop your ball within two club lengths of where the ball last crossed the margin of the hazard, no nearer to the hole. Margins are usually marked with stakes or paint.

OB

When your ball comes to rest in an "out of bounds" position, an area literally outside the boundaries of the golf course indicated by white stakes or other perimeter markings like fences, you're not permitted to play from this location under any circumstances. Under the rules you'd re-play from the place where you originally hit the ball that went out of bounds and add a one stroke penalty to your score. It's called stroke and distance. For example, if you hit your tee shot out of bounds, hit another tee shot, then compute your score as follows: one stroke for your first shot, plus a one stroke penalty for going out of bounds and one stroke for your second shot. Therefore, you'd be lying three after your second shot. You'd follow the same procedure for a lost ball.

The Rule of Equity

If a situation isn't covered by the rules use common sense, but you can't make rules up or agree to waive a rule with your playing companions. The complete *Rules of Golf* are available at most golf shops. If not, ask your golf professional how you can acquire a copy. Like golf itself, you'll learn the rules most easily if you first understand the basics and then take time to study the details.

The only rule you can add to the Rules is the "rule of fun". Enjoy your time on the golf course!

Golf Behavior: Some Dos and Don'ts

Golf is a game of refinement played by courteous players whose behavior shows respect for the history of the game, the playing field and their fellow golfers. Wow, nice sentence.

Here are some guidelines in this regard.

- Don't be a "rule-e", one of those jerks that's always spouting the rules,

Don't get in front of the player hitting the ball.

but on the other hand, don't be unruly either—one of those golfers who is always breaking the rules. Somewhere in between is the junior who plays by the rules and helps others to do the same.

• Don't be loud on the course. Loud talking, shouting and banging about in the cart are no-nos, as is playing music. And please stand quiet while another golfer is trying to play.

• Don't get ahead of the person who's hitting. On the teeing ground stand a safe distance to the side of the player who's about to hit. And never stand directly behind or ahead of someone who's hitting. Wherever you stand, please stand still so as not to distract their eye.

• Do say good shot or nice try where appropriate.

• Do wait to hit until all members of the group ahead have left the area you're hitting to.

• Do yell "Fore" if you hit a ball that looks as if it might land close to someone. Don't scream "four" (fore) at golfers as you drive by the course.

• Do play without delay. Always be ready to play when it's your turn.

• Do watch where your ball goes. It cuts down on the number of lost balls if everyone in your group watches each other's shot and marks where it landed.

• Don't linger by the green to calculate your score when you finish the hole. Go directly to the next tee and write it down there.

• Do leave the bunker by the low side, but before you go, rake it free of your footprints and divots.

Rake the bunker when you leave to make it free of divots and footprints.

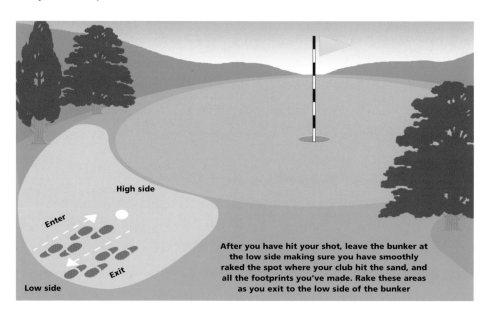

High side

Enter

Low side

Exit

After you have hit your shot, leave the bunker at the low side making sure you have smoothly raked the spot where your club hit the sand, and all the footprints you've made. Rake these areas as you exit to the low side of the bunker

- Do repair your divots in the fairway and rough, and fix your ball marks on the greens.
- Do observe the cart rules just as you do the rules of the road if you drive. In no case should a golf cart be driven or parked too close to the green.

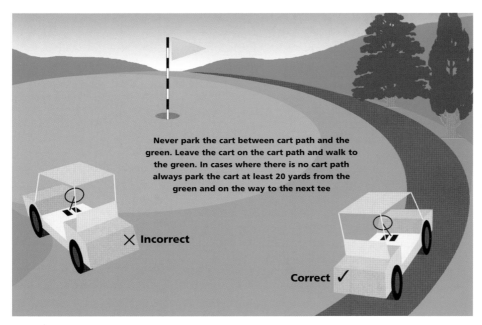

Always leave your bag away from the green (1) and not in the area immediately surrounding it.

Never park the cart between cart path and the green. Leave the cart on the cart path and walk to the green. In cases where there is no cart path always park the cart at least 20 yards from the green and on the way to the next tee

✗ Incorrect

Correct ✓

- Don't lay your bag or park your pull cart on the area immediately surrounding the green.
- Don't walk on the line of anyone's putt including your own and don't drag your feet as you walk around on the green.

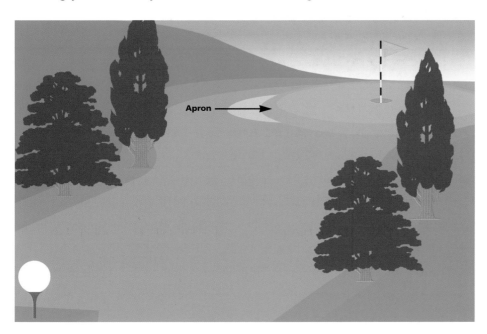

Apron →

Earl Woods—a great influence on Tiger.

3

On Teaching Your Junior

Don't Make It Too Hard and Do Make It Fun

If you have a child this will come as no surprise to you: kids love to play fun games, so if you want them to learn golf the first principle is make it fun. You know that golf is a great game, one your kids can play for their whole life time and that exposure to the game and the type of people who play it can teach young people valuable lessons. As Earl Woods, the wise parent of golf phenomenon Tiger Woods, has said: "If you as parents can teach your children to love and respect the game of golf, they will inevitably learn important lessons about life."

The Game of Golf is Worth It

Golf can be used for relaxation, enjoyment with friends, competition and later for business, and you can play it long after the ability to play soccer, baseball, basketball and football are gone. You know this, but the chances are your kids don't, hey they're busy sliding into second base or worrying about the school prom, so how do you let them discover the long-term advantages of golf without being too pushy? In other words, how do you motivate your kid to play golf?

Motivation

Motivation is not innate, i.e. you're not born motivated. It's a learned skill, and that's an important point because it means that kids can learn to be motivated. What certainly helps to motivate them is when they see you doing something with golf, like bringing them out with you when you play and practice. Kids are great copiers and with the advent of Tiger Woods they now have a role model for golf, so that in addition to wanting to "be like Mike" they now can imagine "I am Tiger Woods".

Modelling

There is no doubt—your kids will model you. The greatest golfer of all time, Jack Nicklaus, copied his dad, who carried a single digit handicap. Phil Mickelson's father was a low-handicap player and used to bring Phil to the practice range in a bassinet so he could watch him hit balls. The same is true of Tiger Woods whose father would sit young Tiger in a highchair while he hit balls into a net. Both Nick Faldo and Greg Norman modeled their mothers who were fine players. It's the same with many other famous golfers—they got their start watching their parents.

But what if your swing isn't good enough to serve as a model? Our advice is to make a video of a good swing, let your child watch it so they can imitate it, then give them feedback on how close they're getting. Over time they'll get closer and closer to matching the model you've chosen. Note that you're not giving lessons, but you are serving as another set of eyes that helps them with the proper feedback as they copy their model.

Two Types of Motivation

There are two types of motivation: motivation to avoid failure and the

What His Father Taught The Tiger

TIPS

1. Earl was Tiger's model. He tells of the time he first realized that Tiger was something special. He would sit in his highchair and watch his father hit balls into a net. Then he wanted to try. At ten months old he hit balls left handed. "One day," Earl remembers, "in the middle of his swing, he abruptly stopped, walked around on the other side of the ball, changed his grip to a right-handed grip and hit the ball as if nothing had happened."

2. Tiger learned that golf was fun and it was something that gave him an excuse to tag along with his beloved father. At two years of age, Tiger had memorized his dad's work number and just before quitting time, Tiger would call and ask, "Daddy, can I practice with you today?" What fun for the both of them and what a way to develop a wonderful relationship.

(Continued overleaf)

**What His Father
Taught The Tiger** *cont.*

TIPS

3. One early lesson Earl taught Tiger was the importance of a pre-shot routine. Earl asked Tiger a very simple question; "Doesn't every shot start with a target?" When Tiger said yes, Earl then asked, "What better way to determine your target than to stand behind the ball and look at it?" Tiger, then three years old said, "Daddy, you know that's right. That's a good idea." And he's done it ever since.

4. Earl, almost a scratch golfer, taught Tiger the basics, but when it was time (Tiger was four), he sent him to a professional instructor. "Paramount in the selection of Tiger's mentor," wrote Earl, "was my decision to stand in the background and let the two develop a relationship. Support is much more productive than interference."

5. Most important of all in our opinion, is that Earl taught Tiger that he cared about Tiger first and Tiger's golf second. As Tiger lay in his crib, Earl would repeat over and over: "Daddy loves you. I am here for you. Daddy is so proud of you. I want you to be happy." And that was long before the agents, the money and the glory.

motivation to achieve success. Although both work in shaping behavior, we believe the most successful for golf is using success as the motivation for learning the game rather than the fear of failure. So it's up to you to instill in your young golfer the proper relationship between failure and success. Kids want to please you by doing well and the way you respond to their failures and successes will determine how they feel about themselves and about golf. To do this, structure the learning so that at each point success is rewarded, while failure is treated as an inevitable part of the process of succeeding. There are three ways to get this point about failure across to your kids: tell them; show them; praise them.

1. Tell them about what we are talking about here—they'll understand. No golfer likes failing, but it's part of the game just as hunger is part of the enjoyable process of eating a delicious dinner and a boring car ride is a necessary part of a fun vacation. Babies learn to walk by falling down and during the learning process, falling is not failing, rather it's a valuable learning tool. Later on, once the skill of walking is learned and you flunk your sobriety test and fall down at the feet of the officer who just stopped your car, then falling is a failing that will land you in jail—and rightly so.

2. Show them how you handle success and failure in your own behavior. How young golfers look at failure will influence both how well they learn and how well they play once they get to the course. Kids often react to failure in the same way their parents do and if you treat failure as a disaster so will they. If they see you get upset over a missed short putt or a shot that goes in the bunker, then they will learn to fear failure perhaps so much that they may even quit the game. So if you play golf with them, make sure you show them, by example, how to fail correctly. Remember you're a hero to your kid and she or he wants to be just like you, so how you act, they'll act.

3. Use praise when they succeed; praise them when they hit a good shot, set goals for them when they practice (e.g. knock in five three footers in a row) and when they reach the goals, give them an enthusiastic "well done". We all thrive on stroking and no young golfer ever

suffered from too much legitimate praise (they'll see right through false praise so don't use it, it will just confuse them). If you frame it correctly that old bogey man of failure can be turned into a birdie and actually used as a stepping stone to their best golf.

Please remember that kids are always making judgments about their abilities in relation to other kids. If you make golf too difficult by accepting nothing but perfect execution before praise is given, kids are liable to judge their abilities to be less than the other kids and this will often cause them to lose interest in the game.

How To Make It Fun

It bares repeating that the best way to teach kids is to capitalize on their natural inclination to learn through play, so rather than making learning a set of axioms about the golf swing, make it a game and kids will learn it much faster that way. Hands-on teaching techniques, like games and drills, make the learning atmosphere interesting. You can arrange chipping and pitching contests, or trick shots like hitting balls on one leg, or hitting shots with your entire body facing away from the target at address. The key is anything that's different will keep their interest.

Hey Dad/Mom, How Should I Feel About Myself?

Your junior may never ask you this question, but chances are they're thinking about it, so it's essential to make sure that they don't relate failure to their self-esteem or self-worth. How good they are as a person should not be hitched to how well they strike a golf ball. In basketball you can run down the floor without touching the ball, your teammate can swish a jump shot and you win because your team won. If he misses, you can convince yourself that your team lost, but the loss wasn't your fault.

In golf, however, there are so many opportunities to personally fail (like on every shot) that if the kids think it makes them worthless to fail, the game of golf becomes an agony. If you show tremendous disappointment when they fail, it will put a lot of pressure on them to succeed—far more than you might think. This kind of distress can take all the fun out of the game. Golf should be enjoyed because of the nature of the game rather than used as an instrument to get something else like recognition for you as the parent of a star golfer, or money down the road or a scholarship in two years.

Mastery, Competitiveness or Both?

Mastery implies that your goal is to improve your skills, so that your grip, posture and ball flight are getting better over time and it is this kind of improvement that drives you. The competitive aspect is framed in terms of how you're doing against other players—are you beating people? Golf has both a mastery element and a competitive element and the balance between the two is key to your junior's development.

The research shows that age is important when kids are considering which goals to pursue. Under the age of 12, they are more likely to focus on mastery as a goal—they want to be able to "do golf " for themselves like they do video games. After age 12 three general classes develop: some kids become very interested in the competitive aspect of golf and mastery becomes a necessity for winning—it's simple, the better you hit the ball, the more kids you'll beat; others kids remain interested in honing their skills, they want to play the game well and don't care too much for competition; the third group just want to compete. They never practice and don't care much about their swing, they live to be involved in tournaments. The point is that within golf both the competitive and the mastery goals exist, and it depends on your child's personality and their age as to how she or he will balance the two.

Growth and Patience

Somewhere around the age of seven, sport-related movements become possible for the kids. (In gifted motor phenomes like Tiger Woods it's earlier, but that's unusual). This is important because growth influences performance and movement. As a child grows, changes in height, weight, muscle mass and limb length, combined with a lowering of the center of gravity, markedly affect performance and not always for the better, at least in the short run.

It's hard to establish habits that direct the junior's swing pattern when the particular skills they've practiced are related to a golf season. Their body changes during the off-season and when they come back to golf, they have actually "switched bodies", so the information they learned

They're Not All The Same

TIPS *Like anything else you have to know the personality of your kid. If they are a loner, golf is a great game because they can go off by themselves and practice. If they're shy and sensitive about people watching them when you take them to the range, don't plunk them down in the middle of everybody. Arrange it so they can practice or take lessons in a place where there isn't a bunch of people watching. On the other hand, there's nothing better than practising with a pal, so if you're going to the range let them take a companion along. And while they're there for mastery, don't be like the jailer at a boot camp—within the bounds of propriety, let them fool around and have fun.*

The parent/child relationship is so important: be like Earl Woods, who was always in the background for the young Tiger.

must now be matched to a different body: different ratios, different lever length and different balance points. Just re-calibrating the timing of all the parts to the new body is a task. Knowing this helps us understand the temporary performance decrease noted during growth. Obviously it's hard for your juniors to maintain their skill level when they're growing like a weed, so you should explain that the "two steps forward, one back" is normal as they learn golf. This way both you and your junior can be patient as you wait out the growth spurts.

Start Young

It appears to be the early experiences in childhood that lay down the neural tracks in the brain which are compelling in adulthood, so the common advice to start young comes as no surprise. *In Why Couldn't Michael Hit It*, a book dealing with Michael Jordan's inability to hit a baseball at a professional level, the author, a neurologist, states that there are brain programs necessary for playing any complicated sport. These programs are made up of inter-connections of brain cells that tell you how to do something like hit a golf ball, and they take a long time to develop and are best laid down when you're young. Jordan had a basketball-wired brain, but as great an athlete as he is, it was too late to start all those new neuronal pathways in his thirties when he decided to give big league baseball a try.

Our advice is to introduce your juniors to golf as early as you can by letting them model you, but hold the formal training (the three phases outlined below) until after the age of seven.

Three Phases to Learning Golf

Phase One: Understanding the Concepts

There are three phases in learning golf (or any motor activity). First, the junior needs to understand conceptually what they're about to learn—not perfectly, not even in minute detail, but enough so that they have a grasp of why it's important. Let's say you're teaching your junior the grip and you've presented the perfect grip you want them to copy; you might say something like this. "The grip (how you place your hands on the club) is the only contact you have with the club. Think of it this way—your hands are the clubface, meaning that whatever your hands do, the clubface does as well." As you demonstrate by rolling your hands back and forth to show how the clubface rolls back and forth, too. "If your hands are wrong, your clubface will be wrong at impact, but if your hands are right, your clubface will be looking directly where you want your ball to go, so the ball will go straight." And it registers in the young learner's brain—"So that's what a grip is—no wonder it's important—hey, this is worth learning."

While You're Helping Them, Please:

1. Don't talk down to them—give them a chance to hear adult sentences. Kids grow in their ability to handle intellectual concepts and golf is a great way for them to practice their new-found abilities to use their brain.

2. Don't talk louder to make your points, they're young not deaf—and please don't whisper as if they were still in their crib

3. Don't talk at them— you're not dispensing the wisdom of the ages, you're sharing some guidelines with them. Your partner(s) will learn much more quickly if you have conversations with them rather than lectures.

4. Don't be a wind bag— help sessions should be no longer than 30 minutes with ten minutes of talk and 20 minutes of doing.

(Continued overleaf.)

Phase Two: What Causes What

In the first phase of learning, the young golfer understands how the club is actually swung and they set about learning the motions that send the ball to target. In the second stage, they are concerned with figuring out how those motions (the takeaway, the right arm fold—all the motions described in the chapter five) are related to an outcome: what contact feels like; seeing the ball rising from the turf; and the look of the ball flying through the air. It is at this point on the learning curve, where concept meets execution, that "Aha" experiences take place at such a rapid rate that all you need do is stand back and let it happen. "Hey," your learner thinks, "If I grip it like this the ball goes one way and if I grip it like that, it goes another way." By the way, this is definitely no time to recite from "the scrolls of instruction", the aged swing wisdom passed down to you from the 30-handicap golfer who lives next door. It is a good time for you to stand quietly and simply observe the wonder of a perfect learner learning perfectly.

The place to learn the what-causes-what of the golf swing is on the practice tee where kids link the concepts to the actual movements necessary to make a complete swing. Simply stated the program is as follows—give your kid some ideas of what they should be doing, show them a model of how to do the stance, grip, takeawy etc., then give them a pile of balls and let them have a go at it. If they have trouble, bring them to a good teaching professional who will help them with their mechanics as they match the model.

Phase Three: Golf vs Golf Swing

The final phase is to be able to do the golf swing without thinking about it. This is the where the swing has become habitual and you don't have to think directly about the individual parts of it. Young players may have a swing key, but instead of thinking about the function of the left knee and the right elbow as they might have when they learned the game, when they play the game, they must learn to focus on the target. In other words they need to play golf not the golf swing.

Every One on the Same Page

So tell the kids what the program is, and that way you'll all be on the same page. Explain that first they are going to learn the concept, (for example,

While You're Helping Them, Please: *cont.*

TIPS

5. If you don't know what you're doing find a good teacher for your junior— if you're a hacker who can't break 100, give your support rather than swing advice. And a few lessons for His-Self wouldn't hurt either.

This last one we see violated all the time on the driving range. Think about it for a second—would you take advice from your doctor about how to give up smoking if he had a cigarette hanging out of his mouth? What is the impact on your young learner if, after you explain how to hit the ball correctly, you turn to your pile of range ball and fire off three grounders, two or three bone-jarring fat shots and finish off your demonstration with a series of banana balls that even your 300 wide range can't hold?

what makes a good grip or why the takeaway is important). The human brain loves concepts and once your young learner has an idea of exactly what it is they should be doing, it makes it a lot easier for them to actually do it. Next comes the "how to do it" part of the learning where you provide a model for them to match. Learning to swing a golf club is the same as learning any other grouping of movements dedicated to produce a specific result like tying your shoe laces or driving a stick-shift car. Thinking about what to do while you do it, ruins your performance (execution), but as soon as it becomes a habit and you can do it without thinking about it, your results improve dramatically. Once they can match the model you have presented to them and can do it reasonably well, it's time to practice until it becomes a habit. When they can swing without thinking about it, it's time to go play golf.

If kids understand the stages they will be going through, much of the problem of unhealthily high expectations can be avoided, especially if they know that when they get to the automatic stage, they're going to take a big step up on the performance curve. The answer to the question, "Why can Johnny hit the ball so good and I can't?" goes something like this: "Remember we talked about the steps you'd take to learn golf—well Johnny is at step three and you're at step two and here's what we have to do to get to step three."

It's a Partnership

While you are the teacher you're also an equal partner in your child's learning experience. It may be your knowledge, but it is their experience, so it's a partnership of sorts and if you treat it as such, your kids will both love and respect you—and the two are different. As Tiger's father, Earl Woods has said: "The parent must understand that love is given and respect earned."

The Set Up

We define the set up as grip, ball position, posture, stance, aim and alignment. A proper set up is the best thing you can give yourself, because it helps you make good golf swings that are the same every time. Think of it this way: if you kept making different turns to get to your house, you'd get their some of the time but you'd get lost a lot of the time and it's the same way with your swing—always take the same route to the ball and you'll have a consistent swing you can rely on.

The other advantage of a proper set up is that it encourages good balance as well as correct swing mechanics. We have found that a bad set up is the cause of most swing flaws, no matter what your level of play; as a matter of fact, over 90 per cent of all swing errors can be traced to a faulty set up and the sad fact is that for every set up error you commit, you'll have to make up for it during your golf swing.

The importance of set up makes good sense if you think about it—golf is a game of geometry (lines, arcs and relationships), so how you hold your golf club, where you aim the face, how you position your body in relation to your target and where you put the ball in your stance controls where the ball goes. Now what's your new, most favorite subject in school? Geometry right.

When you set up to the ball correctly, you have the right geometry and your odds of making a good swing dramatically increase. The good news is that, to make a good set up, you don't need any special athletic talents or previous golf experience. Once you know the details of a good set

A good set up is crucial for a good swing.

up, you can put yourself in a position that gives you the best chance to make a good swing every time you address a ball. If you use the guidelines that follow and repeat your set up until it becomes a habit, each swing you make will be set up for success.

Something to Remember

Before we start, here's something you should keep in mind as you learn your set up: while you're building your swing piece by piece, don't confuse comfort with correct. When you're learning something new it never feels right at first. Actually it's backwards—it feels good to do it wrong and it feels bad to do it right. Say you have a very poor posture at address—you're all slumped over with too much on your toes. Then you learn the correct posture, knees slightly flexed, weight on the balls of your feet and bent a bit from your hip joints. To anybody who knows anything about golf you look a lot better, but your brain is telling you how bad you feel. So which do you listen to, your brain or your teacher? If you listen to your brain you're a goner. To get better, you'll just have put up with feeling uncomfortable for a while—how long? It varies, but this uncomfortable time is an "incubation period" and in learning any skill it depends on how perfectly you do it and how many times you repeat it before your new skill becomes a habit.

And while we're handing out advice, how about this: when you're learning to make a golf swing, don't let the ball be your master. It's real easy to change something in your swing after a bad shot—that's what we call letting the ball control you. When the ball is your master you make changes in your swing based solely on how much you liked the previous shot, but when you use the ball flight (high, low, slice, hook etc.) to tell you how well you're learning, you'll spend most of your time tinkering with your swing trying to get the ball to go straight rather than learning each piece of your swing, one at a time.

Remember, when you're learning a swing piece (for instance the grip) your evaluation system for success is how well you're matching the model grip, not where the ball goes. You might have six more changes to make in your swing before you can expect the ball to go where you want it to, so don't use ball flight just yet.

Grip

Your hands are your feel center and more than half of the nerve endings in your body are located there so they're sensitive. Try typing with gloves on and you'll see what we mean. Here we're going to repeat something we said before because it applies in spades when it comes to changing your grip: the first hurdle in learning a golf grip is not to mistake what's comfortable with what is actually correct. Like anything new, a correct golf grip may not feel comfortable at first, but because it supports your club throughout your swing, coupled with the powerful action it allows in your wrists, it's paramount that you stick with the correct grip.

Variation vs Mistake

Since your hands are your only direct connection to your club, the importance of taking your grip correctly is obvious. Look at some of world's best players—they don't all hold the club the same way, but there are some ways that you can put your hands on the club that just don't work. Grip variations such as the grips that Lee Trevino, Paul Azinger or Jim Furyk use, match the rest of their swing, but that's quite different from the mistakes that can be made when you put your hands on a golf club any old way. The bottom line is that variations are one thing, mistakes are quite another.

One of the worst mistakes to make is to place the club handle too deeply into the palm of either hand. Though this grip may feel ok, it provides little support for the club during the golf swing and allows the club to bounce around out of your control. This kind of bad grip also restricts the wrists to the point where they don't work very well and that causes a loss of power. If you learn to play golf with this mistake, you'll develop a chopper's swing, because your faulty grip forces you to lift the golf club up with you arms without coiling, and all you can do is come down like you were chopping wood with an axe. When your grip is correct, however, it helps you "swing" the club and elevate it with the turn of your body and the cocking of your wrists. So let's get to the basics and later on you can add your own variations.

Placement of the Left Hand

Rather than placing your hands on the club with the clubhead soled behind the ball and well below your hands, hold the club up in front of you to take your grip. Extend your right arm fully in front of you, and place the club in your right hand with the shaft at a 45 degree angle to your body (see, here's that geometry again). Now extend your left arm to meet the club, making sure that your left arm is resting on your chest and

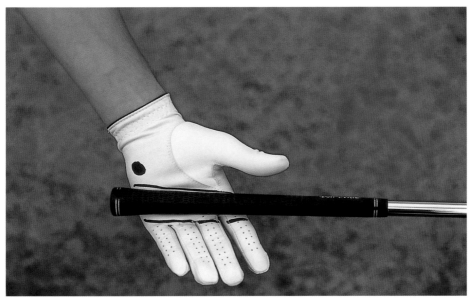

Placement of the left hand: run the handle of the putter across the bottom of the palm.

Note how the "V" on the player's glove points to his right shoulder.

run the side of the handle across the bottom of the palm of your left hand. Don't try to make the grip end run diagonal with your hand open, it will be that way only after you close your left hand around the club. Make sure that your left thumb ends up to the right of the center of the grip, so that the top of your left hand looks more towards the sky than the target. How much does the top of your left hand face the sky? Well, it varies, depending on how strong you are and it can range all the way from slightly (that's called a weak grip and to use it you need to be strong as a garlic milk shake), to a lot (a strong grip).

The best way to find out is to experiment; once you get all the elements of your swing in place, hit a bunch of balls over a couple of weeks and see what happens to the ball flight when you weaken your grip as opposed to when you strengthen it. In fact, you should do this kind of customization with all the parts of your swing, one at a time, to see which variations are right for you. Our advice is that you wait to do this until your swing is completely installed in your brain.

Placement of the Right Hand

Keep your grip on the club with your left hand and with your left arm extended, rap the two middle fingers of your right hand around the handle and stick your right little finger straight out. Slide your fingers down the shaft until they contact your left hand. Now close your right palm over your left thumb. Your right index finger

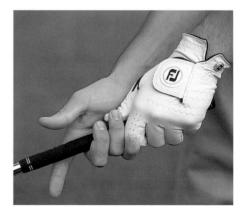

Right hand shaft across second knuckle.

curls around the club so it lightly touches the tip of your thumb. Finally close your pinkie around the knuckle of your left index finger and there you have your starting grip. We use the term "starting grip" to make the

Both hands are placed on the club— note how the knuckles are aligned.

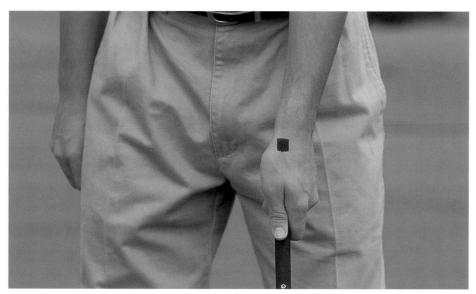

Use your snuff box (marked) to ensure that your left wrist joint is directly on top of the club.

Note how the heel pad rests on top of the club.

point that your grip may well change as your swing develops, but you've got to start somewhere and this is a pretty good place to start.

Other Kinds Of Grips

The grip we describe above is not the only good one and if you just don't want to do it this way, there are a couple of others you might try. The "interlock grip" is so called because you intertwine the right pinkie and the left index finger: they wrap around one another. The interlocked fingers should meet at about your knuckles to maintain the club more in the fingers of each hand. If you choose the interlock grip be careful not to intertwine these fingers so that the base of your palms touch each other. One of the dangers of this grip is that its easy to do it wrong and force the club too high into the palms so that you can't cock your wrists correctly. Still, how bad can it be if Tiger Woods, Davis Love and a lot of other tour players use it?

The ten finger, or baseball, grip can be effective if you have limited strength and/or trouble cocking your wrists. There are two kinds: the first is the true baseball grip with your left thumb wrapped around the handle like the rest of your fingers (just like you hold a baseball bat). This is not recommended because with your left

The two V's are parallel.

Your Guide to a Perfect Grip

TIPS Locate the two tendons of your left thumb by keeping your arm quiet and moving your thumb toward your body. Look just below your right wrist and you'll see an area with a depression called the snuff box. Use this as a guide to insure that your left wrist joint is directly on top of the club rather than to one side and adjust your snuff box until it's directly over the center of the handle of your club. (See above). Check to make sure that the heel pad of your left hand, (not the thumb pad), rests on top of the grip. You should feel that the club lays across the second joint in the fingers of your right hand. Make sure to fit your left thumb into the pocket formed by your right thumb pad and heel pad. If you've done this, the palm of your right hand aims parallel left of the target.

thumb off the handle, you loose the support you need for your club at the top of the swing. The other modification of the ten finger grip occurs when you curl nine fingers around the handle and extend your left thumb down the right side of the shaft just as you did in the overlap grip. This is a good alternative if you're into the ten-fingered variation.

Choosing a grip is mostly a matter of personal preference, but, regardless of the type of grip you use, be sure to test it against the check points for a good grip.

Grip Pressure

When your grip pressure is too tight you can't cock your wrists enough to make a powerful swing. If you strangle the club, you cut off all feel to your brain and it doesn't know what to do. Your goal is to cock your wrists correctly and that means you make a straight line formed by your left arm and the club shaft at address into a 90-degree angle by folding your wrists so that your arm and club shaft are now perpendicular. It's the same in hockey or baseball—without this L-shaped angle all you can do is make a weak slap at the ball.

Now once you've created this angle of power you need to keep it until just before impact, and here's where the correct grip pressure is so important. With the proper grip pressure your brain will make the adjustments necessary to maintain the correct hold on your club as you swing. All this is done automatically and if you try to hold onto the club you'll no doubt overdo it and freeze your wrists so they can't work like they're supposed to. We like the term that expert teacher Chuck Hogan uses; he calls it a "hold" rather then a "grip". Your pressure should be light enough to allow you to cock your wrists enough to create the L, but firm enough so that you don't have to re-grip during the downswing. On a scale of one to ten, where ten is a death grip and one is much too light, your hold on the club should feel like a five. We'll contunue to use the word "grip" becasue it's the standard, but we want you to think of it in terms of a "hold".

Posture

To establish good posture, take your grip on the club and stand tall with your arms straight in front of you and the club shaft horizontal to the

**Strong Hands,
Strong Swing**

TIPS

Strong hands and forearms are important in golf and it's easy to make them strong by squeezing something like a rubber ball while you're watching TV, riding your school bus or listening to a lecture in English class. If you forget your ball, just press your index finger and thumb together and hold, then push and hold the last three fingers of each hand against the palm of that hand. Do it now and feel how you work your forearm muscles.)

The perfect posture sees the knees flexed so that they are over the shoelaces (2). An incorrect posture will see the player either too upright (1) or too bent over (3).

ground, then simply let the clubhead drop to the ground as you bend forward from your hip sockets. Now flex your knees slightly until you feel balanced. Don't push your knees too far out toward the ball—a good guide is that your knees should be flexed so they're over your shoelaces.

Note that it's your hips that bend your upper body forward, placing your weight on the balls of your feet, but it's your knees that bend your body backward until your weight settles across the arches of your feet. So the correct mixture of knee flex and hip bend distributes your weight from the balls of your feet back through your arches. When you've done this correctly, your rear end sticks

The perfect posture: everything is aligned.

A few posture drills: (1) Bend your knees; (2) with your legs locked, stand with the shaft on your hips; (3) with your buttocks out, tilt your spine forward.

out behind, acting as a counter balance to your head which, because your spine is at an angle to the ground, sticks out over your foot line. Check this out in a mirror: if your posture is correct you'll see that an imaginary line connects the top of your spine, the tips of your elbows, tips of your knees and the balls of your feet. Remember your weight should be distributed from the middle of your feet to the balls of your feet—never out on your toes or completely back on your heels.

Stance Width

How wide you spread your feet in your set up affects your stability, balance and mobility and the distance between your heels varies according to the length of the club you're using (always use your heels to measure, rather than your toes). You also know that the longest club in your bag is the driver and the shortest iron is your wedge. You probably already know that the length of each of your irons varies by $1/2$ inch, so that means that you will be closer to the ball with your short irons and father away with the woods; and while there is no iron-clad rule, basically as you move closer to the ball, your stance narrows and, as you stand farther away, it widens.

Note the difference in set up between the player with the driver (1), the mid and long iron (2) and the short iron (3).

See the different ball positions between a driver (1) and an iron (2).

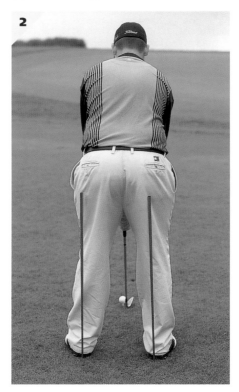

Don't try to be exact regrading your stance width because junior golfers have different widths depending on build, strength and flexibility. Here is a very general guideline you can follow though: when it comes to your long irons (four, three or two), fairway woods and driver, your stance should be a shoulder width apart to accommodate the wider swing arc that the shaft length of these clubs demand.

When you're using your medium and short irons (five–pitching wedge), your feet should be about the same distance apart as the outside of your hips. Because the medium irons (five, six, and seven) are longer than your shortest irons, your stance will be a little wider than your hips, while your width with the short irons (eight, nine and wedge) will be slightly less. The important thing to be careful about is how to measure your foot spread. As we've said, the correct way to measure is from heel to heel rather than from toe to toe. You'll get fooled if you flare your feet outward and use your toes as a guide. Since you can't see your heels, it's easy to keep them only a few inches apart and not know it, a common mistake that gives you too narrow a platfoem to support the movement of your body throughout your golf swing.

To be sure your stance width is correct, use the following test. Take what you think is the appropriate stance and hit the ball, holding your follow through so you can check your finish position. If your knees end up even with each other, your stance width is correct. If there is a large gap between your knees your stance is too wide and if your right knee passes your left, your stance is too narrow.

Foot Flare

If you stood at address with both feet pointing straight at the target line, you would have no flare at all. How much you should turn your feet out at address depends on your ability to turn back and through the ball. Some juniors will have

Start off with a $^1/_4$ turn foot flare.

very little flare and some will have a lot. It depends on how you're built in the hip area and every one is a little bit different. The average flare is about one quarter of a turn from perpendicular and you should start by stepping in with your feet pointing directly at the target line, then turn them out 25 degrees.

By itself, your foot position is the least important of the body alignments, but one of the most important for power because at impact, the left leg must act as a wall to hit across just like a home run hitter in baseball. Basically your left foot controls the timing of your release of the clubhead to the ball (this is called "impact"): to make the release later, increase the flare, to make it sooner, decrease it. Your right foot flare controls how much you'll turn away from the ball.

Ball Position

Impact is also determined by where you position the ball in relation to your body and your ball position depends on what club you're using. With your medium to short irons (five through to pitching wedge), play the ball off your left cheek so that it's position is slightly forward of the center of your stance. Using your feet as a guide as to where to play the ball can cause some mistakes because its hard to judge exactly where the ball is in relation to your feet when they're flared, so it's best to use your upper body to make sure you've got the position correct. As we've said, for your short irons it's off your left cheek. For your long irons and fairway woods, off the logo of your shirt on the left side of your chest, and with all teed woods including driver, play the ball opposite your left arm pit.

Use the aiming lines on your clubface to line up the ball to the target.

Aim and Alignment

When your body is parallel with the target line, it's said to be square to the target. When your clubface points directly to the target, it is also square. And you thought being square was bad? The key here is to begin all normal full shots from a square set up position with regard to both your clubface and your body. Now this may sound too simplistic, but it's your clubface that makes contact with the ball and where it's looking at impact determines the direction and spin on your golf ball—two pretty important elements in hitting good shots. As simple as aiming would seem, though, and as easy as it is to actually do—how hard is it to aim your clubface correctly?—far too many juniors mis-aim. So here's the secret of aiming: use the lines on the toe and heel formed by the groves on your clubface and take great care to aim your clubface at the target at address, because that's where you want it looking at impact.

Getting Hip

A special note: watch what you do with your hips at address. The alignment of your hips is important because they control the amount of rotation away from and back to the ball. If you let your hips get open (pointing to the left of the target) the chances are that's how they'll be at impact too and the ball will fly off to the right of the target. If your hips are closed at address, you run the risk of over-turning on the backswing and then not being able to get your hips turned back in time for impact forcing you to overwork your hands and hit shots to the left.

If your hips are too open (1) the ball will fly off to the right; too closed (3) and the ball will go to the left. Square hips are the secret (2).

Your Shoulders

Because of the way humans are built, your arms, if left alone, swing naturally in the same direction as your shoulders, so make sure your shoulders point to where you want the ball to go. Actually your shoulders should be parallel to the target line just like your hips. Juniors, like their adult counterparts, often make the mistake of aiming their body lines at the target instead of parallel to the left of it. In this case the clubface usually aims to the right of the target and the body is in a closed position. When your aim and alignment are wrong, you've got to make a bad swing to hit a good shot because when you're aimed to the right, your swing path is too much in-to-out and the reverse is true when you're open (aiming to the left). To make sure that your aiming procedure is correct, you need a good pre-shot routine.

Your Pre-Shot Routine

We'll introduce the concept of a good pre-shot routine here and give you the particulars in Chapter Seven on tournament golf, because when the pressure is on and your mind is racing, the ability to make the correct plan, build a good set up and make your best swing when it really matters is what makes you a good tournament player. In this chapter, we want to make the point that the process you go through to hit a golf shot brings together all the aspects of your set up that we have discussed so far, especially your aim and alignment. If you're diligent about building a good set up, you'll also develop a strong pre-shot routine, because the elements of your set up become so "routine" that there's no chance of forgetting something.

When you practice, go through the process of building your set up exactly the same way for each shot you hit in practice—always make sure that you take the same amount of time for the routine. Before you know it, you won't even think about taking your grip, your stance, posture or ball position and this frees your focus what really matters—the target. If you hurry and break your pre-shot pattern, you'll probably end up hitting a bad shot. A good routine, from the time you tee the ball until the time you hit the ball, should take no more than 30 to 45 seconds. If you take longer than that, you are slow and you should redo the time frames for your routine.

Full Swing

The Perfect Golf Swing—A Bad Idea

It's not helpful to talk as if there were one perfect golf swing hidden away somewhere, an idea that implies that to play good golf all you have to do is find it. This kind of thinking makes learning the golf swing a lot like looking for buried treasure. You search and search and because you don't know exactly what you're looking for or how to find it, you go down a lot of blind alleys and waste a lot of time.

Rather than "finding" something, we see our junior students as "building" something. We think learning the golf swing is more like constructing a building, where you follow a blueprint: first you put in place a good foundation; then you add one room at a time; and when your house is done you live in it as a home—it's a comfortable, complete unit that exists as a whole rather than just a group of separate rooms.

Learning a golf swing is like learning any other sequence of movements. First you need to understand what it is you're trying to do when you swing a club and then it's best to have a model, something or someone that you can copy, a blueprint that serves as a guide as you build your own golf swing. Then you need to put each room in place, the stance, the takeway etc., until the blueprint is completely filled out. And now comes the hard part—once you get it built by blending together the individual pieces of the swing, you must put Humpty Dumpty back together again—forget the pieces of your swing and go play golf.

In what follows, we've described the entire swing in piece-by-piece detail based on our belief that your golf swing will be no better than your concept of what a good swing should be. As teachers we have said this for years and will say it again to you—if you know what to do and it's clear and distinct in your mind, then you'll be able to do it.

The swing mechanics presented in this section give you the information you need to build your swing, but we cannot stress strongly enough that this information is not for thinking about while you're actually playing the game. The idea is to develop a golf swing that you don't have to think about. With this in mind, you are now ready to construct the blueprint for your golf swing and we begin with several key concepts that apply to all golf swings, no matter how personalized.

14 Clubs, One Swing

As we saw in Chapter One, your clubs have a progression of increasing loft along with decreasing shaft length, so your driver looks quite different from your sandwedge. And it's only natural that because the clubs look and feel so different, many juniors think they need a different swing for each club. Actually you need only one swing, regardless of the club you're using. As you have already learned in Chapter Four, your ball position and stance width changes when you change clubs, while your set up and swing are fundamentally the same with both. Since your woods are longer, you'll be further away from the ball, but the relationship of your club to your body never changes when you adhere to the principles of good posture.

What changes, without any effort on your part, is your swing as you progress from long clubs to short. For example, since your driver has a long shaft and you're naturally farther from the ball, your swing plane is flatter (more around you). At the other extreme, your short-shafted sandwedge puts you close to the ball and therefore your swing plane is

Don't Be Discouraged, You're Just Growing

TIPS

Adults are pretty stable when it comes to growing, so they don't have to worry about their body changing right in the middle of learning a golf swing. But kids grow. You get taller, wider and stronger and this is important because your growth influences how you perform. So lots of things change as you grow including your center of gravity and your limb length. This can make it hard, because the things you learned to do six months ago may no longer match your body. This is why you often see fluctuations in performance and you'll have periods where you can't do what you thought you had already learned to do. It's hard to keep your skill level with timing and power when you're growing like a weed, and both parents and kids should understand that. So don't get too upset when you take some backward steps—be patient, it's only temporary and you'll grow out of it.

steeper (more above you). The key is to make a good set up and swing, letting the design of the club dictate the changes in your swing.

The Swing Itself

The Takeaway

There are two things that you need to do during the takeaway and they happen together—your left arm must swing across your chest while your right hip begins to turn over your right heel. Remember that your weight is shifting into your right hip, establishing it as a pivot center. Be careful here because it's possible to turn your right hip without putting any weight on it, a common mistake that leaves the weight in the left hip creating a reverse pivot, i.e. you've turned your hips, but your pivot is wrong.

With this in mind and taking care to begin from a proper set up position, you're ready to start your takeaway—the movement of the club away from the ball. Good golfers have initiated the takeaway in a number of ways and while it's not written in stone, we recommend that you let your left arm swing across your chest until it begins to pull your left

The takeaway: the left arm swings across your chest until it pulls your left shoulder behind the ball.

The takeaway: just before your hands reach hip level your wrists will begin to cock.

shoulder behind the ball. As your left arm swings, your right arm moves away from your right side and your right elbow moves down your toe line the same amount as your left arm moves across your chest. This creates a small, but noticeable, window of space between your right hip and your right elbow. Just before your hands reach hip level, you'll begin to cock your wrists. When you do, your hands remain low as your clubhead raises high and slightly behind your toe line.

From a well-executed takeaway position you'll start to feel coil building in the muscles of your left side, especially the back of your left forearm. As the motion of your left arm across your chest drags your left shoulder away from its address position you'll also feel coil as your weight shifts into your right hip.

Three Cautions

Caution One: Your right elbow should float down your toe line and it must remain pointing down that line. It should not be allowed to move inside your toe line

Coil builds as your weight shifts to your right hip.

The club plane should pass through the target line (indicated by row of tees) with the right arm parallel.

Tee in butt of club.

The left thumb points to the sky.

because if it does, your hands will go where your elbow points and the clubhead will swing too far behind you. To control the clubhead as a junior player, you have a strong left-hand grip and the correctly positioned elbow prevents you from turning the club too quickly inside, which is always a danger with a strong grip.

Caution Two: In addition to letting your right elbow swing too far inside your body line, another common error during the takeaway occurs about waist-high if you roll your hands and forearms so that your right palm looks at the sky. This causes your clubface to open too early and the clubhead swings to much behind you. From this position your only option is to lift the club to the top, destroying your coil and the path of your swing. The solution is simple—keep the back of your left hand pointed at the target line during your takeaway. To help you do this, hook a golf tee to your golf glove at address and complete your takeaway so the pointed part of the tee aims in the direction of the target line.

Caution Three: You may have heard of the "one piece takeaway" recommended by some instructors, but unless you're very strong we want you to stay with the advice given here. The one piece demands that you start everything (club, hands, arms, shoulders and chest) together away from the ball, but if you're not careful, you'll turn your hands and club inside your toe line too quickly, ruining your coil and fouling your swing plane. This is why we recommend a sequence of moves starting with your left arm during your takeaway and then a one piece "upswing" where your club is elevated to the top of your swing by simply turning your chest while you fold your right elbow. At this stage of your development, the left-arm takeaway is much safer and produces more coil.

Set The Wrists

At the end of your takeaway, your wrists should cock so that your thumbs point at an angle to the sky; when you do this correctly, the shaft of your club forms the same angle with the ground that it did at address, i.e., the butt end of your club points at an extension of your target line back from the ball. With your hands on your toe line, your clubhead is now high but your hands are still low, about level with your waist. The club should now be in a very light position supported by the pedestal of your hands. You're now ready to elevate the club to the top of your swing by folding your right elbow to form a right angle between your forearm and your upper arm.

To The Top

There is a wrong way and a right way to get your club in position at the top of your swing. The wrong way is to consciously lift your arms, an error that destroys your coil and timing and results in a loss of distance and accuracy. Here is the correct way: from your completed takeaway position elevate the club to the top of your swing by continuing your shoulder turn as you fold your right elbow. In doing so you'll build maximum coil, maintain your posture and keep your swing on the track.

The shoulder turn continues as the right elbow folds, building maximum coil.

The right takeaway creates the perfect swing plane.

Understanding Your Shoulder Turn

To be sure your shoulders turn properly you'll need to keep them moving at a 90-degree angle to your spine. To understand how your shoulders work, stand in front of a mirror and you'll notice your shoulders form a "T" with your spine when they are level to the ground. Now bend from the waist into your golf posture and turn your shoulders. If you keep your spine angle the same, and simply rotate your shoulders, the left will go down under your chin and the right behind your neck and this is exactly the shoulder motion required for your golf swing. The idea is to keep your shoulders perpendicular to your spine as they turn both back and through the ball without changing your spine angle.

The key here is that you don't make any effort to move your left shoulder down to the ball, a swing error known as "a shoulder tilt", where your spine angle changes. When you tilt your left shoulder down, your weight stays on your left leg and never gets behind the ball. Another temptation is to level your shoulders to the ground as you turn in your backswing. This straightens your spine and destroys your posture.

Hip Turn and Weight Shift

As you can see, your backswing is controlled by a combination of arm swing and shoulder turn, but there are several other important elements. Your hips play a significant role in the backswing, moving in response to the motion of your upper body. Your hips turn until your right hip is over your right heel. Depending on what club you're using, at the top of your swing you should feel between 60 (short irons) to 80 per cent (driver) of your weight in your right hip with the weight balanced from the ball of your right foot to your heel. To avoid a lateral hip sway, keep the weight more toward the inside, rather than outside of your right foot.

Downswing

At every golf seminar or golf school we give, we get the same question—
"How do I start the downswing?" While there are many ways, depending
on the way you're built, in general we recommend the following. The
start of your downswing requires two moves performed simultaneously:
led by your shoulder, your left arm falls back down your chest as your
weight shifts from your right leg to your left. Just as your left arm swung
across and up your chest to begin your backswing, it now reverses its path
to start your downswing. Note that we didn't advise you to force or pull
your left arm down, you let it come down. Your left arm will follow your
left shoulder—as it moves up during the downswing, your left arm moves
back down across your chest.

The weight shift from your right to your left side goes with your arm
drop, and after it's accomplished your hips take over your swing and begin
a powerful rotation, with your left hip serving as the center for the
rotation. Again, this transfer of weight is a subtle movement similar to
shifting your weight when dancing.

*Downswing: your left arm falls back down your chest as your weight
shifts from your right leg to your left in a reverse of the backswing.*

Downswing: the clubhead is on a collision course with the ball. Note that as your left arm moves forward, your left leg straightens to provide a wall to hit against.

The Hip Sway

Trying hard to transfer weight to your right side, it's easy to sway rather than turn your hips. When the hips sway they move laterally, to such an extent that the right hip slides outside the right leg. On the downswing, the left hip slides too much toward the target so that it is outside the left leg through the hitting zone. The problem is that while all this sliding is going on, coiling and the correct swing path take a back seat, so when you sway your hips you'll hit a variety of fat and thin shots. To be sure your hips are working correctly, plant a shaft or an umbrella next to the outside of your right heel and take your backswing. If you sway, your hips will bump into the shaft, but when you turn your hips, your right hip moves behind you so it's over your right heel—you won't touch the shaft.

Contact

When your downswing unfolds as it should, your clubhead is literally on a collision course with the ball. Your arms move down your chest and back in front of you, and your shoulders key your swing motion just as they did in your backswing. Your left shoulder moves forward and upwards away from the ground and your right shoulder moves toward the place your left shoulder occupied under your chin at the completion of your backswing. The rotation of your left hip moving behind you causes your left leg to straighten, providing a firm wall to hit against. At impact, your clubface mimics its position of address. As you swing through the ball, your

Arms and shoulders still rotate after impact.

arms and club whip past your body at a high rate of speed, a result of your body rotating around your left hip joint. In order to stay balanced, your spine tilts slightly away from the target (usually about five degrees), so that you can "stay behind the ball"—the hallmark of every good swing.

Chin Behind the Ball

Keeping your head behind the ball is a key to a powerful swing, but don't confuse this with the advice "keep your head down",

Impact comes at the centre line of the body.

because the two are very different. You can keep your head down in your golf swing, but that doesn't guarantee you'll stay behind the ball at impact. So forget "keep your head down" and focus instead on keeping your chin pointing behind the ball until your right shoulder pushes it up after the ball is gone. When you allow your head to be drawn up as your shoulders turn through the ball, you can complete your golf swing and finish in balance.

After the Ball is Gone

Even though your follow through happens after the ball is gone, it's an important part of your golf swing. After impact, let your body rotate upward around your spine without any feeling of restriction in your left or right side. Allow the force of your right shoulder turning through impact to gradually rotate your head toward the target so that you're looking "under" the ball as it flies away. In other words, allow your body to fully release through the ball, neither adding anything nor holding anything back—whatever is moving, keep it moving. A good player finishes with his head, chest and hips facing the target and all of the weight on the left side. The back foot is almost completely off the ground, with the toe acting as a rudder for balance. Even if the ball doesn't go

Over The Top

TIPS

A move called "coming over the top" that gets many juniors in trouble, occurs in the transition from backswing to downswing and it can happen even from a good position at the top. It's pretty normal to want to kill the ball, but the problem is you don't want to do it at the start of your downswing. When you do, your hands and your right shoulder, instead of moving down, move out towards the ball, pushing your clubhead well outside the path you established in your backswing. In addition, your left arm is forced away from its powerful connection to your chest, leaving you with a side-swiping action that cuts severely across the ball. So have some patience up there and let the downswing happen, don't make it happen.

After the ball has gone allow your body to fully release through the ball. A good player will finish with his/her chest, face and hips facing the target and the weight on the left-hand side.

where you want it to, practice finishing each swing in this fully released and balanced position. And every time you finish out of balance, take a practice swing and concentrate on returning to the correct position.

One of the advantages of a good finish is that you look like a player and if you do it enough, you will be one. A good follow through is a result of what went before, but if you train yourself to go to that position after each swing, you'll help the earlier parts of your swing. When you know where you're going, you'll use the proper muscles and movements to get you there.

The perfect follow through.

Summary

As you've probably noticed, your downswing is a reverse of your backswing. To review, your left arm swung across your chest and your wrists set the clubhead up and slightly behind you as your weight began to shift into your right hip. When your arm could swing no further, your shoulders began their rotation around your spine and to swing the club to the top, your right elbow simply folded as your shoulders continued their turn. To start the downswing, the motion reversed itself. Following your left shoulder, your left arm moved back down your chest as your weight shifted to your left hip, a trigger that started your left hip moving behind you. Your clubhead released to the ball and, after impact, your wrists re-hinged with your left elbow bent. Your posed finish had four basic elements: 1. Your weight was on your left side; 2. You were standing at your full height; 3. The front of your body was pointing at the target including your right knee; 4. You were up on your back toe, using your back foot as rudder.

Advice To Beginners

TIPS

Almost all beginners (except you of course) try to lift the ball off the ground and into the air. They hang on their right side with no weight shift during the downswing and flip their wrists to try to "get under the ball". Now while it makes sense that you'd swing up to get the ball up, it is actually just the opposite—you swing down to get the ball up in the air. So their effort produces exactly the opposite objective: either they catch the top of the ball and hit a grounder, or they hit way behind the ball and produce the dreaded fat shot. You don't do anything to help the ball into the air because the loft of the club is designed to do that for you. Instead of trying to drive your ball up, your goal is to drive the ball forward to the target, letting the loft of the club provide the "up".

Grip It, Rip It and Worry About Finding It Later

Most major league baseball scouts look for young pitchers who can burn the fastball. They figure that they can teach a kid to throw the curve and you can teach control, but you can't teach them to throw hard. And it's the same with golf. We believe that kids should always learn distance before accuracy. If you learn accuracy first you'll never be a long hitter. It's much better to have a hard swing and learn to control it later than it is to worry about control first.

And along these lines, you'll often hear "let the club do the work". Be careful how you interpret this advice. If you take it to mean that the cub will somehow generate its own speed, this concept can seduce you into making too easy a swing. To hit it far your golf swing needs to produce high clubhead speed with solid contact, so learn to go after the ball. The point is that a powerful golf swing is neither dainty nor magical. It's physics; contracting muscles and strength coupled with technique— so learn aggressiveness first and control later.

The basket drill: an aid to hand-eye coordination.

Drills

The Basket Drill

The simple drill to enhance your hand-eye coordination is to toss balls into a basket. Stand six feet from a wash bucket and toss balls into it. When you can make eight out of ten, take two steps backward and repeat until you are 20 feet away.

The Patty Cake Drill

Choose a partner and face each other in your golf posture (be careful not to bang heads). Each junior extends their right hand so that their palms are facing one another. From this position, take turns gently swinging your right arm back and through as it would in your real golf swing, so that your palm meets your partner's at impact. This is great for your hand-eye skills

Takeaway Drill

To be sure you have a perfect takeaway, lay a club shaft on your toe line as a guide and keep your hands over the shaft during your takeaway. When your left arm reaches a position where it's parallel to the ground, check that your hands and your clubshaft are still on your toe line directly over your guide shaft.

Arm Stretch Drill

Place a ball on the ground and, without using a club, bend from your hips while kneeling on both knees (put down a towel so that you don't get your pants dirty). Grip an imaginary club with your left hand, then hook your right hand underneath your left elbow (the palm of the right hand should be facing the target). From this position, simply pull your left arm across your chest until your left shoulder is pulled behind the ball. This drill lets you get used to the feel of the proper sequence—left arm first then shoulders and because your lower body is fixed since you're kneeling, you can feel the coil developing.

Pump Drill

The pump drill gives you the feeling of the club moving down rather than around to start the downsing. Start this drill from the position at the end of your takeaway, where your left arm has swung across your chest and your wrists have cocked the clubhead at about waist high. Now turn to the top of your swing and pump the club gently up and down several times and on the third pump, hit the shot. You'll feel how the upper and lower body combine to bring the clubhead down to the ball.

Delay Drill

During your downswing, your arms need time to drop, and this drill teaches you to delay your right-side turn back to the ball just long enough to give your arms time to drop. To get the feel of this delayed right side, exaggerate the flare in your right foot to 50 degrees. Hit balls doing this drill. Note that while your weight shifts to your left hip to start the downswing, your right side doesn't start to rotate until the club drops down.

Adjustments for the Female Junior

There are some adjustments that female juniors can make to improve their swings. In general, girls have more flexibility, less muscular strength, especially in the upper body, and a lower center of balance than boys. Below are several specific recommendations based on these differences.

Ham It Up

Often the muscles that support the knee located behind the thigh (the hamstrings) are not as strong as the quadricep muscles in the front of the thigh. This is why many girls lift their heels off the ground during the downswing, a move that shoves the weight suddenly to the toes, throwing the whole body out of balance. If both heels come off the ground during your downswing, we recommend that you do exercises to increase the strength of your hamstring muscles. And to be sure that you're distributing your weight correctly during your swing, practice hitting balls with your toes curled. This will encourage you to distribute your weight from the balls of your feet to your heels.

The Overswing

A long, high arc is a great way to produce distance, but only if the club is in control. When the club is out of control, the swing produces off-center hits which actually lesson the distance, because when you hit the ball outside the sweet spot (the center of the clubface), you can lose a lot of distance. The problem is that it's easy for girls to over-turn because they are more flexible than boys in their hips and knees. If you're extra-flexible and you swing way past parallel, point your right foot to target line to help tone down your over-turn. This limits your hip turn, but still allows you to turn your shoulders so you can build a lot of coil.

Another reason for the over-swing, where the clubhead dips way past parallel, is because the left arm bends during the backswing. This happens when, instead of turning your shoulder behind the ball at the top of your swing, you lift the club up with your arms and hands without coiling. If you take care to make a complete shoulder turn, with your flexibility, you can keep your left arm straight (not stiff) and swing the club under control to the top of your swing.

Forearm Strength

Junior girls may have strong quadricep muscles, but their strength is not as great in their forearms and hands. Therefore you have to focus to make sure you're aggressively releasing your forearms, i.e. letting them rotate through impact. Many juniors don't release fully because they hold the club in a death grip and guide it into the ball. So first make sure your grip is correct (*see* below) and then be sure to let your forearms rotate through the ball. It's also a good idea to squeeze a soft, palm-size ball and if you're 16 or older, do some very light forearm curls to increase the strength of your forearms.

The Grip

When you take your grip with your left arm at the side of your chest and the clubhead resting on the ground, the club shaft is diagonal to the body and it's very easy to mis-position the handle too high in the palm of the left hand. And, as you reach down to take your grip, it's all too easy to dip your right shoulder down and out toward the ball as you put your right hand on the grip.

To avoid both problems use the following procedure to grip the club. With your right hand, hold the club in front of your chest at a 45-degree angle to your body. Extend your left arm out to meet the club, making sure your left upper arm is resting on top of, rather than beside, your chest. Assume a strong left-hand grip, so that when you sole the clubhead behind the ball, the back of the left hand points toward the sky and the palm of your right hand is facing the target.

Summary: The Golf Swing is Dynamic

As we have said, in order to describe the details of your golf swing it's necessary to break them down into individual pieces so you can learn them. Please remember, however, that your actual golf swing is a dynamic motion and cannot be executed piece by piece when you are on the golf course. As you can imagine, while you're actually swinging, it would be impossible to think about even a few of the many instructions you've learned about the golf swing. So while your swing can be learned one piece at a time on the practice tee, when you play, you'll need to stop thinking in pieces and let your motion be a fluid, continuous swing.

And it works the same way when you're fixing your swing, as you will have to do from time to time after you learn it. What you need to do is evaluate the area of your swing that is troublesome and work on that one piece until it becomes a habit. Be sure to eliminate errors in your swing in the order in which they occur. For example, fix a takeaway error before you work on your downswing. Golf swings are an excellent example of

TIPS: Once you've placed your right hand on the club, check it by simply extending your right index finger down the shaft. If it lines up directly behind it so that the shaft is between your finger and the target, you're fine. If the finger is on top of the shaft, your right is too weak; if it's under the shaft, it's too strong.

cause and effect, so often you'll find that an error late in your swing disappears once you perfect an earlier part of your swing. And this follows through to your set up—most errors are eliminated once you set yourself properly to the ball.

Junior Model Swings

The swings that follow are sequences of good junior golfers, but they are not the polished swings of tour players and many of them have some flaws. However, all of the players featured here have tournament experience and while all can break 90, some can break 80—and some come pretty close to par. In any case, all of them have good enough swings to serve as general models. In some instances we have repeated our descriptions or made very similar comments from model to model because there are certain themes in a good swing that keep repeating.

Swing A

Frames A1 and A2

These two frames teach the importance of coil. Compare them and you can see what we mean when we advise you to coil for power. In frame A1 this junior is almost at the top of his swing, yet his hips and left knee are almost in the same position as they were at address. His coil potential is huge because he is turning the top of his body against the bottom. In frame A2, he's reached the top of his swing and both his hips and left knee have finally turned because they could no longer resist the pull of his upper body. He's about as wound up as you can be and that spells power.

Frame A1

Frame A2

Frame A3

This frame shows that the downswing starts with an unwinding of the hips rather than the hands or shoulders. Note how our model starts the downswing with his hips by comparing his belt buckle in frame A2 and this frame to see that his hips start his clubhead back to the ball. Also compare the position of his clubhead in both frames—it's on its way back down in response to the hip action.

Frame A3

Frame A4

Here is a classic photo that shows what we mean by "staying behind the ball". Note how the folds in his pant legs billow out toward the target. This shows that his left side has provided a firm "wall" to hit against. He's in the correct lower-body position at impact because his upper body has tilted slightly back away from the target in response to the momentum of his arms swinging past his body. Note his head and spine in relation to the trees in the background in frames A2 and A4, allowing the slight upper body tilt away from the target necessary to stay behind the ball.

Frame A4

Frame A5

The full extension of both arms shows that there was no slapping with the hands. And look at how he keeps his head back where it was at impact, this is insurance that under pressure, he won't slide forward through impact with his upper body.

Just after impact his arms are in front of his body because he keeps his head behind the ball creating a whip-like release of the stored energy. Notice how his left arm is still connected to his chest guaranteeing that the power generated by the rotation of his trunk and hips is transferred from his body to his arms and then through the shaft into the back of the golf ball.

Frame A5

Frame A6

As with the rest of his swing, his follow through is textbook. You could see the spikes on his right shoe if he was wearing spikes. His belt faces the target as does his right knee. This perfect finish is simply a result of what went before.

Frame A6

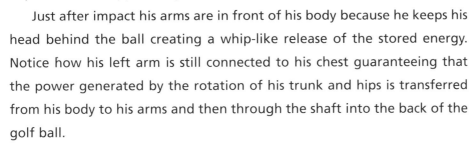

Frame B1

Frame B2

Frame B3

Frame B4

Swing B

Frame B1

At address he has assumed a perfect posture position with the shaft and spine at 90 degrees to each other. With the exception of his knee joints, all the load-bearing joints are aligned with each other. The top of his spine, the tip of his elbow, and the balls of his feet are all in alignment. This means he needs a bit more knee flex to put him in perfect position—the guideline is that your knees flex until they're over your shoe laces.

Frame B2

Waist high, the left arm and wrist are still straight and the toe of his club is pointing to the sky with the shaft parallel to the ground over the foot line. None of the height the clubhead has attained at this point is due to wrist cock. This is the end of the takeaway and from here the arms stay close to the body, and the club is set in position at the top of the swing by folding his right arm.

Frame B3

At the top of his swing his elbows are level and if you draw a line connecting them, they form a perfect triangle with the clubshaft at the highest point on the triangle, running parallel to the target. As we'll soon see, all he has to do is to keep the triangle intact and drop it to the ball. Take special note of his clubface—it's at the same angle as his left arm. This is called a "square clubface" and it's one of the best things this young golfer does in his swing.

Frame B4

Starting down the triangle formed by a line connecting his elbows, he tilts so that the clubshaft moves more to the left of the target before it drops downward. This moves the shaft across his right biceps, a position called "on plane" because the shaft is at the same angle at this critical juncture as it was at address. The dropping of the triangle into this position is accomplished by the correct action of his lower body. His weight transfer to his left side and the rotation of his left hip are the key. Note that he has increased the flex of his knees to get into an athletic position necessary to smash the ball. It's a good compensation, but as we have already said, it would be much better to have done this at address than to try and reflex your knees while you swing.

Frame B5

Frame B5

This frame captures him just before impact with the triangle still intact. He has a terrific amount of right knee drive, keeping his right foot pretty much planted late into the downswing. And since he's kept his hands out of the swing, he's able to retain the 90-degree angle between his left arm and the clubshaft—this is "tour-like".

Frame B6

His left knee comes straight just before impact, slinging the club across it like a home-run hitter in baseball. The extension of his clubhead away from his body creates maximum width, a position attained only by a very good player. From bottom to top, this position looks great—the sole of his right foot still looks at the ground and his head is behind the ball.

Frame B6

Swing C

Frame C1

He is in a good athletic position to swing the club except we'd like to see him with a touch more knee flex. He shouldn't squat, but, as we've said above, his knees should be over his shoe laces. It's as bad to squat as it is to have too little flex. Remember the knees are designed to bend the body backward not forward, and if you bend from your knees instead of from your hip sockets, you'll ruin your posture.

Frame C1

Frame C2

His takeaway ends with a folding of his right elbow that sets the clubhead well behind him, but allows his hands to stay in front of his chest. He keeps his right elbow pointing to the ground, a move that, when coupled with some left forearm rotation, points the club shaft at the proper angle—one that matches the shaft angle at address.

Frame C2

Frame C3　　*Frame C4*　　*Frame C5*　　*Frame C6*

Frame C3

His arms continue to swing back and up, causing the shoulders to turn on an incline at right angles to the spine (the spine is the axis for the shoulders). Once his wrists have set correctly, all the relationships he needs to complete his backswing are in place. Now all he must do is to continue his turn. Once again the angle of his clubface matches his shoulder angle.

Frame C4

He starts his downswing to the ball with a lateral motion of his hips towards the target. This slots the club shaft behind him so he can come to the ball on an inside path. About half way down when his left arm is parallel to the ground, his right knee begins its kick toward the target, while at the same time the left hip turns to the left. The right elbow gets closer to his body without the right heel flipping up and out toward the target.

Frame C5

Through impact his left hip has rotated behind him, increasing the pulling force on the clubhead. When your hips rotate correctly, it feels as if the clubhead is whirling by you and the release just happens—in fact, you can't stop it. To get this whirling feeling try this: wait till there's no one around and practice throwing clubs by letting them fly out of your hands just before impact. To do it correctly you must rotate your left hip behind you, just as you should in a real swing. By the way, this is the only time you should ever throw a club.

Frame C6

The spine is upright but tilted a bit to the right with the right shoulder slightly lower then the left in a sideways "C". The club shaft runs through his ears, but since his head is slightly tilted, the club shaft is diagonal with the ground.

Swing D

Frame D1

Frame D1

The right shoulder is under the left by the same amount that her right hand is below her left on the club handle. Because she is so flexible, her feet are almost perpendicular to the target line to place a governor on her turn. The ball is well positioned off her left cheek.

Frame D2

She starts the club away as the text suggests, by letting her left arm swing across her chest with the toe of her clubface pointing at the sky. Note that her left arm does not roll during the takeaway. The latter (a forearm roll) fans the clubface out of position. She keeps her left elbow pointing at the ground so she can swing the clubhead away from her with maximum extension and without fanning the clubface open.

Frame D2

Frame D3

In this frame our young junior gets the club into a light position at the end of the takeaway. She controls the golf club by setting her wrists, using her hands as a pedestal to support the weight of her club. Now by simply folding her right elbow and continuing her turn, the club will reach its position at the top. (Not shown here.)

Frame D3

Frame D4

The right side stays back as the left shoulder moves out from under the chin and the arms drop the club first downward and then forward toward the ball. The club must move down then around, never the reverse (never around then down). Once this is done, her right side rotates back to the target, thereby delivering the clubface square to the target at impact. Note her right knee starting its kick—it leads the right side into the ball.

Frame D4

Frame D5

Frame D6

Frame E1

Frame E2

This junior could increase her distance by retaining her wrist cock longer. As you can see in this frame, she has lost the angle between her left arm and club shaft too early and created a power leak. Compare this position with frame 5 in our B swing to see the difference. As she gets stronger, she'll be able to hold the angle longer, but she also needs to rotate her hips behind behind her more to keep the power angle.

Frame D5

Her left arm is against her chest giving her the left arm-to-chest connection necessary for accuracy. Her chest is looking at the ball with her arms and hands in front. She could use a bit more hip turn here, at least to 45 degrees. When the hips are turned 45 degrees out of the way, the left leg straightens creating clubhead acceleration and while her left leg is straight in this frame, it was a little late in getting there.

Up on toes—let's repeat what we said in the text. Often the muscles that support the knee located behind the thigh (the hamstrings) are not as strong as the quadricep muscles in the front of the thigh. This is why many juniors, especially girls, lift their heels off the ground during the downswing, a move that shoves the weight suddenly to the toes, throwing the whole body out of balance.

Frame D6

Her follow through shows she has recovered quite nicely into a beautiful finish. Her hips are fully turned, her chest faces left of the target and she's perfectly balanced.

Swing E

Frame E1

At address, the club shaft, left arm and shoulder form a straight line with the butt of the club just to the left of the center of his body, almost opposite to the inside of his left thigh. Both feet are slightly flared to make it easier to turn his right hip over his heel on the backswing and to clear his left hip over his heel through impact. When he gets to be 30-something the flare will increase, but for a few more years minimal flare is all he needs.

Frame E2

His arms swing back creating left side stretch and he begins to coil. His shoulders haven't moved much, but the right hip has turned over the right heel establishing the right side pivot point—the point around which his lower body will turn during his backswing.

Frame E3

Note how level his hips are at the top of the backswing and how his left shoulder is behind the ball. His lower body is anchored with the upper body coiled against it. The arm swing creates the width of his swing and his hands are in position over the right shoulder. Even at maximum coil, his left heel is on the ground and his knee is pointing ever so slightly behind the ball, creating the stretch that pays off in clubhead speed at impact.

Frame E3

Frame E4

His head stays behind the ball as he starts his downswing while his left hip begins to turn back over his left heel. His left arm slides down his chest, dropping the club into position. The club has been slotted for the inside approach to the ball with his left arm against his chest, a powerful, connected position.

Frame E4

Frame E5

Through impact he's nicely behind the golf ball. His right heel hasn't flipped up, showing that he has allowed the right side to release, but that he hasn't twisted the right shoulder up and over the ball. He's on his left side, indicating a correct weight transfer.

Frame E5

Frame E6

In his finish position you'll see no wrinkles in his right shoe, indicating he has fully released all his weight to the left. This is a very good swing.

Swing F

Frame F1

Note the perfect 90-degree angle between his lower spine and club shaft as it points to his belt buckle. This maximizes his consistency, because a

Frame E6

swinging object has the potential to move its fastest when it spins at 90 degrees to its axis, in this case his spine.

Frame F1

Frame F2

Simultaneous with the right hip rotation is the left arm adhering to the chest as it moves across it. You can't allow your shoulders to turn too early during the backswing or your club will swing inside and be trapped too much behind the body. Like the other good juniors featured here, he allows his right elbow to float along the body line. If it remains fixed to your side your club will pivot around it, taking the hands inside the toe line—a difficult position to recover from.

Frame F2

Frame F3

At the top of the backswing both of his feet are flat on the ground with the upper body coiled against a resisting lower body. His shoulders are fully turned and the elbows are level. The clubface is a bit shut, pointing more at the sky, with a slightly different angle than his left arm. While there are a lot of good players who are slightly shut, he could square his clubface by matching the angle of his right arm to the angle of his spine.

Frame F3

Frame F4

In the hitting area he returns the club a bit outside of his body line, which, if the clubface is square at impact, will send the ball to the left of the target. You will notice that his right heel has risen only slightly and that his left hip has cleared, moving left of the target and behind him into a very good position. If he came at the ball just a bit more from the inside he'd be better off, but even so he delivers a free-wheeling blow to the ball that becomes even more evident in the next frame.

Frame F5

The key here is that while your left side, from the knee down, stops to form the wall that you hit against at impact, your entire right side must continue its motion so it can smack, full force,

Frame F4

Frame F5

into that wall. This collision gives you a powerful, well-timed release. Note how well he has done this. Both arms are extended in a full release and the butt of the club is pointed to the center of his body. This is because, while it turned, his upper body has also stayed back behind the ball, allowing his arms to release down the line.

Frame F6

He has finished in a wonderful, perfectly balanced position, with his right shoulder actually closer to the target signalling that he has rotated his shoulders fully around his spine. And look at those elbows—they remind one of David Duval's finish while his knees and feet are identical to Davis Love's. That's a nice combination to have, especially at the age of 16.

Swing G

Frame G1

His posture is relaxed with not much spine tilt, preparing him for the flat shoulder turn that characterizes his swing. He has a big chest and his hands and left arm are not going to get as high as most juniors. There is a nice spacing between his body and the butt of the club, about a fist-with-the-thumb-extended distance away. His chin is up in the "proud" position, so his left shoulder has room to turn under it.

Frame G2

He starts the clubhead back low and wide so that at no time is there any slack in the backswing. Looseness in the back swing ruins coil and causes a weak slapping action through impact.

Frame G3

When his wrists cock, the clubhead goes higher than the hands for the first time. The left arm is on the hip line and the clubhead is high and behind him with the shaft through the biceps. This gives him the clubhead depth he needs to match his flat shoulder turn. If he allowed his hands to cross his hip line at this point, he'd be so inside that his clubhead would be trapped behind him.

Frame F6

Frame G1

Frame G2

Frame G3

Frame G4

Frame G5

Frame G6

Frame H1

Frame G4

He has a short swing and arrives at the top with an open clubface because his left wrist is cupped. And because he hasn't made a full hip turn, his hips are tilted a bit too much. But just as there are golfers who play well with a closed clubface, there are also some who play well with an open clubface open. He looks like he's going to hit a fade from this position which is fine, as long as he expects it.

Frame G5

He starts his downswing by letting his arms fall into a good position and reflexing his knees. His left hip has turned over the his left heel maintaining the coil while the hands move downward and away for the right shoulder.

Frame G6

Boom—this kid is strong and you can almost feel the force of impact. He's an upper-body player rather than a player who uses his lower body to move the club around. He's what we call a hitter rather than a swinger and that's one reason why you don't see as much hip turn and leg drive— he's matching his technique to his physique.

Swing H

Frame H1

The modern rotational swing favors a ball position farther back, and with a six iron it's positioned off our models his left cheek. His arms hang comfortably down and his right shoulder is slightly lower than the left. With the iron, his weight is distributed evenly, but with the driver it changes to 60 per cent on the right and 40 per cent on the left.

Frame H2

Neither his shoulders nor his chest turn until they are pulled around by the left arm as it swings away from the ball. The sequence started by the left arm keeps stretch on the muscles of

Frame H2

the left side, especially his triceps. Although it doesn't look it, at this point his weight is already well into his right hip. This is the beginning of the coil and to maximize it, keep your chest to the ball until the tug of your left arm swing brings your chest around.

Frame H3

Frame H3

At the top of the swing both of his feet remain firmly on the ground giving him a stable base from which to unwind. His left knee points at the ball, but it hasn't moved much from its starting point at address. Check out the differences in the amount of turn between his knees, hips and shoulders. The shoulders turn the most, the hips a little bit less and the knees the least. The differences between the three create maximum coil and, as you can see, this is another junior golfer wound like a spring.

Frame H4

Frame H4

From the top, his weight shifts to the left as the left arm slides back down the chest. In this frame his left arm has dropped the club into position and the left hip has turned behind him. At this point the majority of his weight (about 80 per cent) is on his left side and he's in the process of releasing the clubhead to the ball.

Frame H5

Frame H5

At impact his chest is facing the ball and his arms are back in front of his body. Notice how straight his left arm is—from address till just after he has made impact with the ball, his left arm is always the same length, so the clubhead can stay on the swing arc making this junior a very consistent ball striker.

Frame H6

Frame H6

Good players let the right arm straighten after impact—in fact just after impact is the only time in the entire swing that both arms are straight. When the right arm straightens with piston-like force, it drives the clubhead squarely into the back of the ball. The only way to get into this position is to keep your body rotating through impact with your hands in the middle of the chest.

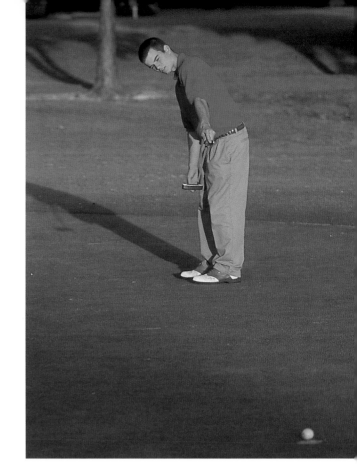

6

The Short Game

Putting

Putting is fun and to be a good putter there aren't a lot of rules. When you watch the tour players it seems that no two of them put quite alike. That's because putting is very individualistic and the main thing is to get the ball in the hole, but there are some things we'd like you to know about putting that will make it easier to find your own style and stroke. Despite its importance, golfers are famous for neglecting their putting practice in favor of hitting full shots on the driving range. There's no question that power and accuracy in your full swing make you a better player, but the easiest and fastest way to lower your handicap is to improve your short game, especially putting. Any way you slice it, and we hope you don't, three of these and one of those adds up to four and the "one of those" is the putt.

Pound a 300-yard drive right in the middle of the fairway, something only a very few can do, and it counts exactly the same as a one inch tap in, something anyone can do. Some great players, like Ben Hogan, thought that putting was too big a part of the game since it accounts for about 40 per cent of the strokes in an average round of golf. Of course, great putters like Ben Crenshaw don't agree, but one thing is for sure, the better putter you are, the more it can save you when your full swing lets you down or your opponent knocks the ball by you off the tee.

Are Good Putters Born?

Some people think that putting is a mystical skill given by the gods, and that great putting is unanalysable. Some even hint that there is a putting genie that confers good putting on its owner. In any case, expertise there is a common misconception that good putters are born not made, another way of saying that you can't learn to putt. Fortunately this is not true. You can learn to putt well and when you do it makes a huge difference in your score. A good example is Gil Morgan, who, while a decent player on the PGA Tour, never reached his potential because he was a mediocre putter. But he worked for one entire year on his putting before joining the Senior tour and he now makes it from everywhere and is winning millions of dollars. So you can get better at putting if you work at it—all you have to do is practice with the proper technique.

A Few Good Ideas On Putting

In all of our books and golf schools we teach putting exactly the same way to juniors, seniors and golfers of every age in between and we repeat it here because it applies to all.

You'll learn three important things about putting by simply clapping your hands in front of you:

1. When you clap your hands they come together as a unit with your palms facing one another and it's the same when you grip the putter. Even though your hands are separated, your palms face each other so that your hands work as a unit—where the palm of your right hand faces so also does the back of your left hand. When your right palm points at the target, your putter faces down the target line.

2. When you clap your hands you also learn where the ball should

be positioned in your stance. Since your hands meet naturally in the center of your body all you have to do is grip your putter and bend from your hip joints until your putter head touches the ground. You'll find that in this position, the handle of your putter points to the center of your body. For the correct ball position simply locate the ball just in front of your putter head and

Position the ball at the center of your body.

you'll have identified the bottom of your swing arc.

3. And lastly, when you clap your hands you learn about the putting stroke itself. Note that in order to arrive together in the middle of your chest, each hand moves at an even, pendulum like pace. This balance is what you want in your putting stroke, so that your putter travels back and through without any attempt to increase or decrease its speed.

The Pendulum Stroke—We Have Ways To Make You Tock

Though there are many putting styles, the one with the fewest moving parts is the most dependable and that's the pendulum motion where your arms, shoulders and putter swing together, back and forth (tick tock). Watch the pendulum of a grandfather clock, and you'll get the idea. The pendulum moves back and forth an equal distance at an even tempo. It never varies from its path because it's fixed at the top and because there is no manipulation, i.e. no one is trying to make it go anywhere, it just swings. Isn't this exactly what you want in your putting stroke? An even-tempo, non-manipulated stroke that remains on the same path back and through the ball. And you can have a pendulum stroke by learning a few fundamentals. Here they are:

Grip

Pendulum putting is a stroke that uses all of the upper body with no wrist action and a very still lower body. This is the motion you use in both putting and chipping where accuracy is king. Therefore it's good to grip the club in a way that quiets your hands so they don't flop around and bat the ball off line. To do this, place the left side of the handle against the life line of your left hand so that the shaft of your putter is in line with your left forearm. Place your right hand below your left, against the right side of the shaft and curl your fingers around with your thumbs on the top side of the putter grip. This lines up the back of your left hand, the palm of your right hand and the putter face, so that they all point in the same direction. It's the goal of your putting stroke to roll the ball to the hole with no wrist action, and the trick is not to change these relationships at any time throughout your stroke.

Placement of the left hand.

Placement of the right hand.

Note the correct posture with the eyes over the ball.

Once you've set your hands on your putter correctly, position your putter face directly behind the golf ball so that it points down the line you want the ball to start on and align your shoulders parallel with, but left of, the target line. Remember that you arms swing on your shoulder line and that your putter is attached to your arms, so make sure your shoulders are correct before you continue with your set up. If your stroke is correct, your putter moves along the target line as long as possible both back and through the ball.

Now check to make sure that your feet are parallel to the target line and that your stance is hip width apart with the most of your weight on the left side throughout your stroke. Flex your knees until your weight is on your heels. You might want to pinch your knees toward each other like Arnold Palmer does so that your lower body won't move during your putting stroke.

The Stroke Itself

We're not going to get you tied up in the mechanics of the stroke because once you have a good set up, the best way to putt is to forget about trying to make your putter "go somewhere" or "do something", but here are a few things you want to work into your stroke no matter how individualistic it is.

1. Feel that there is no conscious "hit" at the ball.

2. Make sure your clubface doesn't slow down as you strike your putt— keep moving at a constant pace.

3. At impact the face should be pointed in the direction you want your ball to start. If your hands are quiet and you keep the top of your spine as the anchor point around which your shoulders rock, your clubface will be square at impact.

4. So now you have the direction for your putt and all you need is the right distance and the only way to get that right is practice.

Jam It or Die It?

It's the oldest one in the book—"never up, never in"—but it's up to you to figure out when to be aggressive. Here your gut feel plays a big role. For any putt you feel you can hole, go at it firm enough to roll the ball a little past the hole. Watch Tiger when he putts those short ones, he bangs them into the back of the hole. Firm putts not only get to the hole, but the firm roll makes the ball less susceptible to spike marks and footprints that inevitably collect around the cup—and when you jam it in the hole you take the break out of the putt so you don't have to worry about it. If you've got the nerve you can plow right through the break and slam dunk it.

Dropping ball on ball: a good drill to make sure that your eyes are over the ball in your set up.

Which Putter?

TIPS *You can't be a good putter unless your putter fits your set up and your stroke. It should be the right length and lie so you can bend from your hips and position your eyes over the ball. When your putter is soled correctly, it should cause your arms and hands to hang comfortably beneath your shoulders. The point is to have your putter adjusted to a good set up rather than adjusting your set up to a poorly fit putter.*

The text recommendations are a starting point for the average junior. For the more advanced junior (almost ready for college), it's time to make some decisions about your putting stroke so that your putter should fit your stroke as follows. If you're a left arm dominate putter, i.e. you want to use your left armpit as the center of your putting stroke, then use a heel-shafted putter and move the ball slightly forward of center. If you're a right arm dominate putter, try a center shafted putter, one with the shaft in the middle of the putter head. How do you know? Experiment with both for several days then choose one and stick with it.

Reading the green: always make sure that you have had a good look at the green before you putt.

How Hard?

Here's a cool way to figure out the speed of your putt. Always take your practice strokes looking at the target. This gives your brain the info. necessary to produce the energy to hit the ball the right distance. On uphill putts, stand behind the ball, farther away from the hole to program a firmer stroke. On downhill putts, stand closer to the hole to program an easier stroke.

If you're good at judging distances you should also be aggressive with medium-length putts. As a good putter, you'll be able to handle the three-footer coming back if you miss the first putt. A lot of playing good golf is knowing what you're good at and staying away from what you're bad at and it's the same with putting. If your distance judgement isn't good, don't try and ram it home—hit a "dying" putt, where the ball trickles over the edge of the cup and into the hole. If you miss, you'll only have a tap in remaining. Regardless of your game plan, make sure that if you miss the initial putt, your next putt is makeable for your skill level. Being aggressive doesn't mean knocking everything six feet by the hole.

Our rule of thumb for you is that putts longer than 20 feet should be played as "dying" putts, as should medium-length putts on very fast or severely undulating greens. With long putts, you must learn to avoid three-putting because there's nothing more demoralizing than to hit the green from the fairway and then to three putt it. Besides, unless you're a Ben Crenshaw with your flat stick, the odds of holing a putt greater than 20 feet are high, so, in keeping with the strategy of playing the percentages, plan on "dying" the ball around the hole on from outside 20 feet.

Putting Drills

Direction Drill

Take two of your golf clubs and lay them down so they form a two-sided track to the hole. Make sure the track is just a little wider than your putter head, so that if you make a bad stroke with your putter you'll know because you'll hit one of the shafts. Now simply place a ball in the middle of your track so that it's about three feet from the hole and putt the ball into the hole. Change the direction of your track about every ten balls or so. The key here is to line up every putt from behind, just as you would on the course, then feel the correct pendulum motion and see the ball go into the hole—time after time.

The direction drill.

Distance Drill

Place three shafts on the green at ten-foot intervals from your ball. Putt your first ball to the shaft furthest from you, 30 feet

The distance drill.

Pendulum motion.

Follow through with firm wrists.

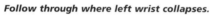

Follow through where left wrist collapses.

Drill: comb on left wrist to prevent collapse.

away. Putt the second ball to the middle shaft, 20 feet away. Putt the third ball to the shaft closest to you about ten feet away. After a few tries you should be able to lay the three balls quite near their shafts. Next putt all three balls to the same shaft until you can putt them into a tight cluster. This drill will teach you how to create the correct distance for your putts.

Pendulum Drill

We've extolled the virtues of learning the pendulum stroke when you putt and here's a very simple drill that will give you the feeling for this type of stroke. Place the grip end of your driver against your stomach about four inches below your shoulder bone. Slide your hands down the shaft to match the length of your putter and align your forearms with the grip end of the shaft. Bend from the hips until your driver soles on the ground. Make your putting stroke keeping the butt of the grip in your stomach and feel your arms and shoulders stroke the ball without any flipping of your wrist. This drill is great for eliminating wrist action.

Chipping

When you're chipping just around the green it's a good idea to chip the ball to the hole with a special technique that will make you a short-game legend once you get it down. Where do you chip from? Our rule of thumb says that even though the amount of rough you need to clear changes for every chip, from five yards off the green and in, you should chip. Once you know how to chip and pitch, you'll be able to tell which technique to use and please remember that five yards is just a general guideline— sometimes you might chip from 30

Five yards off the green and it's time to chip.

yards (down a mound to hard, level ground and low grass) and sometimes you'll pitch from three yards (when you ball is nestled down in deep Bermuda grass). Usually, however, from five yards in, the best shot is a low, running chip shot rather than the lofted pitch shot because it's easier to control a rolling ball than one that flies high.

When you chip you use your putting stroke and since the ball rolls along the green like a putt it's very accurate. And because it's like your putting stroke, you have a good chance of getting very close or even in the hole. Even if you hit a bad chip it usually rolls closer than a badly stuck pitch from the same distance that could put you in the bunker on the other side of the green. Note that you don't always chip from around the green. For instance, you'd putt the ball from just off the green if the grass between your ball and the green is short and the ground is pretty smooth. But if the rough is long or there's something in the way like a bunker, your next choice within the five-yard chipping zone is to chip the ball. When you chip you change clubs the same way you do in your full swing and it helps if you know the flight-to-roll relationship.

The Flight-to-Roll

Time to chip with lots of green.

You don't have to do any math to be a good chipper and after you get the hang of it you'll be able to eyeball the distance and chose the right club, but for now let's understand how changing clubs changes how much roll your chip shots produce.

The key is that you're going to make use of every iron in your bag, depending on the chipping situation you face. Here's another guide line—pick a landing area about one yard onto the green where you want your chip to land and start its roll to the hole—every chip you hit flies in the air a short distance, lands about one yard on the green then rolls to the hole like a putt. Therefore each chip has so much flight time versus roll time. Remember that each of your irons has a different amount of loft, for example your wedge has a lot of air time and little roll and your five iron has a lot of roll and not much airtime.

This table will give you a good idea of how your irons produce air time to roll time.

Time to pitch with no green.

Don't memorize it, but do bring it with you to the practice green and experiment—take a wedge, make a chip and then observe where it landed and how much it rolled. Then check your chart and see if your shot was about one part roll and one part flight. Do this with all your clubs and after a couple of weeks using the chart, you'll know exactly what club to use for your chip.

Club	Flight	Roll
Sandwedge (11 iron)	1 part	1 part
Pitching Wedge (10 iron)	1 part	2 parts
9 iron	1 part	3 parts
8 iron	1 part	4 parts
7 iron	1 part	5 parts
6 iron	1 part	6 parts
5 iron	1 part	7 parts
4 iron	1 part	8 parts
3 iron	1 part	9 parts

Obviously you'll need to adjust the club depending on the slope of the green: chipping uphill—add roll by choosing a five rather than a six iron. If it's downhill—subtract roll by going from a six to a seven iron.

If you're a math-and-measure kind of kid, you might want to choose the club this way using some basic math. It's called a "flight to roll ratio". The flight part of a chip is one part (because you always carry about one yard onto the green regardless of what club you use), versus how many of those roll parts are contained in the distance the ball needs to roll. All you do is subtract how many parts roll it is from the number 12. Here's how it works: say you have a very long chip that you estimate has seven parts roll to the cup once it hits the landing area, here's the formula: 12-7 = 5 so choose your five iron. If you estimated that your roll was six parts you'd choose a six iron, 12-6 = 6; for a chip with twice as much roll as flight you'd choose an ten iron (pitching wedge). To get really good, go to the practice green and throw down a handful of balls and wherever they come to rest estimate how many parts role you have for each ball in relation to the initial distance the ball will fly. Then determine the club by subtraction and hit the shot. It won't take long before you can get it right every time.

Plan Your Chip As If It Were A Putt

Read the green and visualize your chip shot just as you would a putt. You should see in your mind's eye the target line, where you want the ball to begin its roll and also the spot where you want the ball to finish. With the proper club selection and the appropriate adjustments, all you need to think about is how hard you would hit a putt of the same distance. This may sound obvious, but if you're faced with a curving chip, plan it like you would a putt. Set up on the line you want the ball to start on and stroke the chip down this line, allowing the slope of the green to take the ball to the hole.

Chipping Technique

Think of your chip as a putt and make the iron your chipping with like your putter by raising your iron on its toe so the shaft is upright like your putter. This moves you closer to the ball with your eyes over the target line just as when you putt. When you raise any club on its toe, the face aims to the right so take care to turn the toe of your iron in toward the ball until the top line of your clubface is perpendicular to your target line.

Choke down on your iron to make it the same length as your putter and hold it just like your putter. Since you'll use irons of various lengths, this means you'll grip down a lot on the long-shafted four iron and not much at all on the pitching wedge. The idea is to make the various iron lengths consistent with the length of your putter. Actually take your putter and measure each iron to it, placing a band of tape around each shaft so you'll get the idea of how much to choke down while you practice.

There is a question as to what grip you should use because some good chippers use their full-swing grip while others use their putting grip. We think you should use

Chipping is an arm and shoulders motion.

you're putting grip because you're trying to produce your putting stroke while you chip. This way you'll guard against getting floppy with your wrists. For consistency you want to keep your wrists firm and move the club back and through with your shoulders, not your hands, so the chip is a pendulum motion that's controlled by your upper body, with no lower-body and no wrist action.

Set Up

When you're chipping your feet are set close together, because you don't make a weight shift and you certainly don't need power for such a short distance—so the chip requires no lower body motion. When you chip, you want to hit the ball with a descending hit, so anchor most of your weight on your left foot using an open stance where your left foot is pulled back from the target line into an open position where your body points to the left of your target. Don't forget to let your weight settle naturally onto your left foot where it anchors your lower body and encourages your weight to start and stay throughout your stroke. Moving anything that you don't have to move only complicates the shot so stay still with your lower body.

Ball Position

Play the ball back in your stance opposite the inside of your right foot, with your hands set ahead by your left thigh. Your shaft should point at your left shoulder. Lay a club down extending from your right heel to the

There should be no lower body movement whilst chipping.

ball and practice taking your stance. It will look odd at first, but with practice it becomes automatic. You don't try to hit down on the ball because, with your weight anchored on your left side, you produce the proper angle of attack naturally. You want your shoulders parallel to the target line, which means that since the ball is well back in your stance, your shoulders would be closed (pointing to the right of target). The solution is easy—draw your left foot back from the target line until your shoulders are parallel to it.

Stand close enough so that your eyes are over the target line and your arms hang freely, straight down from your shoulders. Done correctly, the ball is close to your feet, generally about six inches away.

The Stroke

Once you've set up correctly, your backswing is all shoulders and arms, without any wrist action. Your shoulders control the stroke in both directions just as they do in the putting stroke. Throughout the chipping motion, your lower body stays quiet, but not rigid. Actually, on longer chip shots you'll need some turn so your arms can swing freely without bumping into your sides, but what movement there is should be reactive.

A common error in chipping is trying to help the ball into the air. To do so, golfers usually fall back on their right side on their through swing to try to get under the ball. This leads to one of two disasters: a fat shot that finishes well short of the hole; or a thin shot that scurries over the far side of the green. To prevent this, practice some chips by placing a board perpendicular to the target line about a foot behind the ball. If your weight is on your right side during the backswing or through swing, the clubhead will hit the board. When your weight stays left, the clubhead never touches the board.

The ball should stay back with the weight forward.

And as in putting, don't flip your wrists around because it changes where the clubface points at impact. Not only does bad wrist action ruin direction, it is also harmful because it adds loft to the club when your left wrist breaks down and the right wrist flips the club under the ball. Eliminate wrist action with the following drill. Place a three iron under your left arm with the clubhead in the air and the grip end pointing to the ground. Join the three iron grip to the grip of a five iron that you'll be chipping with and hold both clubs with a modified grip. If you use your wrists to hit the ball, the shaft of the three iron will hit your ribs. When your wrists are inactive, as they should be, you'll feel the pressure of the shaft against your left arm.

If you've calmed your wrists and used your shoulders in a see-saw motion—left shoulder down for the backswing, left shoulder up for the downswing—your clubface should be still on the target line looking directly at the target after the ball is gone, as if the clubface was trying to "chase" the ball to the target. For a while, check it out after every chip to see that it is. If your clubface is inside your target line, your left shoulder has come around rather than up. If your clubface is outside the target line, your weight has probably tilted forward onto your toes—a sure way to shank the ball.

Chipping Drills

Using your right toe for balance only, hit chip shots with your right heel off the ground and the majority of your weight on your left side. Keeping your weight on your left side insures that contact is made with a descending motion. If your wrists are too active check your finish position. If your weight is on your right side you're forced to flip your wrists to get your clubhead under the ball.

Use the right toe as a rudder.

Shaft under the arm drill.

Shaft Under the Arm Drill

Take an iron and place it across your chest and press down on the shaft with your upper arms so that it's anchored to your body just below your shoulders. The idea of this drill is to chip the ball by moving your shoulders in a sea-saw motion so that your left shoulder moves down on the backswing and up on the through swing. This is the same pendulum-type motion that you use for putting and by using the shaft drill you'll get the exact feel you need to be a good chipper.

Bunker

As in putting, there are a number of ways to play bunker shots—it depends on the type of sand, the position of the flag and your lie. So you won't get confused, we'll stick with the method we teach in our golf schools. It's simple and a good place to start.

Rule one in any bunker is to get out on your first attempt! To do so there are two types of bunker shots that every golfer must learn to play. The first is played from a good lie where the ball sits on top of the sand. The second technique is used from a bad lie, where part or all of the ball is buried in the sand. When the lie is good, play a splash shot. When the ball is buried, play an explosion shot. A lot of golfers fear the sand, and most people call them "traps", but you won't find the word trap in the rules of golf—the hazards filled with sand are termed bunkers and good bunker play starts not only with the right club, but also the right attitude. Where does the right frame of mind come from? It comes from knowing the proper technique and from practicing that technique.

There are a number of ways to play bunker shots.

The dollar bill shows the amount of sand to take.

Shave It Out

You can visualize the splash shot technique if you picture your ball sitting on the center of a dollar bill resting on the sand. We call it the splash shot to emphasize that the clubhead doesn't dig—it splashes into the sand behind the ball. The idea is to slice a thin layer of sand, about the size of the bill, out from under the ball. Your club never contacts the ball, so that the ball rides out of the bunker on a cushion, or splash, of sand. Your sandwedge has bounce, a specially designed bulge in its sole which allows your club to skim through the sand. A correctly hit splash shot sounds like a pop rather than a thud.

Practice with a bounce board.

The Technique

To use the bounce open your clubface ever so slightly (no more than two degrees) so that it points just a bit to the right of your target. Opening the face also increases the loft, so the shorter the carry to the flag, the more you'll open the clubface. Be careful to open the clubface before you take your golf grip and unless you're an expert, don't open it more than four degrees. To do so, aim the clubface to the right of the target (an open position), then take your grip without changing the position of the clubface. If you simply take your grip first and then roll your arms to open the clubface, you won't be able to keep the face open at impact because your arms will roll over as they try to return to their natural position as you swing. Rolling your forearms returns your clubface to the ball in a closed position, just what you don't want when you need to slide your club under the ball.

Point the butt end of your club at the center line of your body, open your stance by drawing your left foot away from your target line enough to re-aim your clubface back at the target—be careful not to touch the sand with your clubhead because that's a penalty. By opening your stance, you encourage your weight to settle on your left side and you'll keep it

Open your clubface so that it points slightly to the right of the target (1). Point the butt of the club at the center of your body and stand slightly farther away from the ball with the ball forward in your stance. Make sure you swing down your shoulder line (2).

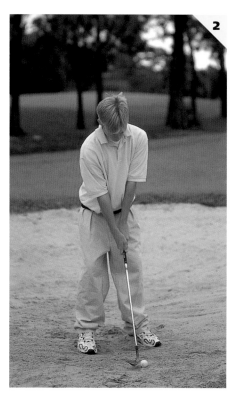

Keep your weight on the left side as you make impact
with the sand (4), and make a full follow through (5).

there throughout your swing, just as you do with all your short green-side shots. This stabilizes your lower body and ensures a descending motion and full finish.

You want to hit the sand shot fat which is why some middle handicappers with steep swings aren't too bad out of the bunker. Since you want to contact the sand behind the ball, position the ball forward in your stance off your left heel. This lets you open your shoulders and, since your club swings along your shoulder line, you're set for an outside-to-in swing path that slices the ball out of the sand.

Dig your feet into the sand to ensure stability, but remember that digging in lowers your feet in relationship to the level of the ball guaranteeing that you'll hit the sand first, a necessary feature of the splash shot. Be careful, though, to stand slightly farther from the ball because, when you dig your feet in, you effectively move the hosel of the club closer to the ball.

The final setup key involves the position of your head—simply keep it in the middle of your shoulders rather than tilting it right or left. Your head can weigh up to ten pounds or more, (if your smart enough to read

Note how the player sets up with an open stance (1) and swings down the shoulder line (2).

This is a wonderfully executed shot.

THE SHORT GAME 107

this it probably weighs a lot more with all those brains), so if you lean it toward your right shoulder, your weight tends to settle on your right side and you'll hit too far behind the ball.

With the weight on your left side throughout your swing most of your motion occurs in your upper body, but don't misinterpret this to mean that you just lift your arms. Let your arms and shoulders swing the club back along your shoulder line and continue this rotation to a full finish.

Outline of the Splash Shot

1. Position the ball forward in your stance.
2. Open your clubface and then take your grip.
3. Open your stance until your clubface aims to the target, keeping the butt of the club at the center line of your body.
4. Stand farther away from the ball and dig your feet into the sand to lower the bottom of your swing arc.
5. Make sure your head is directly between your shoulders and not tilted.
6. Swing down your shoulder line and keep your weight on your left side throughout your swing.

The Buried Bunker Shot—Blast It!

When your ball is buried in the sand, you'll need to explode using a much different technique than the one we have just described for the splash shot. The deal with the blast shot is that it looks tough to get the ball out of the bunker and on the green, but it isn't. The difficult part of the shot is getting the ball close to the flag, because you never know how far your ball is going to run after you've hit it out of the bunker. Even the pros have trouble controlling the distance of this shot, so your goal is simply to get the ball on the green.

To play this shot successfully you'll hit a lot farther behind the ball than you would for a splash shot, but once again, the ball rides out on a layer of sand. Although it varies, most players hit about two inches behind the ball for a regular splash shot, but about four inches to explode the ball. The distance you hit behind a sand shot depends also on the type of sand—if the sand is hard much less, but if the sand is fluffy a good deal more.

TIPS *Even when young players set up directly, it's easy to pick the club up with their arms while their body stays frozen in place. From this position the clubhead comes to the ball on such a steep path that it digs into the sand, often times leaving the ball in the bunker. So make sure to let your chest turn as your arms swing up. One key is to finish in a full follow through with your hands at least shoulder high. You've got to trust your swing to take a full swing for such a short shot, and that's what practice is for—to convince your brain that your technique is correct.*

Note how the weight remains on the left-hand side throughout the shot.

The Technique

The key to getting a buried ball out is a very steep angle downward into the ball, so don't try to lift the ball from this lie. To help you hit down on the ball, position the ball back in your stance toward your right foot. This tilts your spine ahead of the ball and, if you keep your weight on your left side all through your swing, you'll contact the sand at a steep enough angle to pop the ball onto the green. It's also a good idea to close your clubface, to aim it back at your target so you'll expose the leading edge and eliminate the bounce, turning your sandwedge into the ideal club for digging your club into the sand. It's good to use your sandwedge for this shot because it has such a heavy head, but practice a bit with your nine iron, a good choice when you have a lot of green to cover.

Drop your left foot back from the target line to anchor your weight onto your left side. From this position, swing the club along your body line using your arms and hit down behind the ball aggressively. There is one other thing—make sure that while you leave your weight on your left side, you simultaneously turn your shoulders and chest. This turn with no shift plus a closed clubface and a descending blow ensures that your club digs into the sand causing the ball to come out running onto the green.

Since your club buries in the sand, forget about your follow through. But remember that forgetting about it and trying not to follow through are very different. Basically don't try to restrict it artificially because it should happen naturally—your club won't go anywhere if you just let it dig.

Fairway Bunker

Fairway bunker shots are hard for the average junior player because they try to get too much out of the shot. The fairway bunker requires a special technique combined with good common sense as to club selection. And this is important enough to mention right at the start: unless you're an expert, never use more than a five iron in a fairway bunker. Long irons hit the ball too low and fairway woods are too long to handle in the bunker. Both choices create too many possibilities for error, so stick with your middle to short irons from the fairway bunker.

The set up for a shot out of a fairway bunker.

Club Selection

Junior golfers often dread the fairway bunker shot—mostly they get too aggressive and pay the price. Though the shot itself isn't difficult, most problems occur when the conditions of the shot aren't properly evaluated. Before making your club selection, there are a few things you should consider: first check the lie of your golf ball; then the height of the bunker's lip; and finally the distance to your target.

The lie of the ball determines the type of shot you can play. If you have a poor lie, where the ball is sitting down in the sand, take your medicine and select a short iron like a nine iron and hit the ball back to the fairway. If you have a good lie, where the ball sits up on top of the sand, check the lip of the bunker. The lip determines what club you'll need to clear the lip and since the last thing you want is to leave your shot under the lip of the bunker, give yourself plenty of leeway. If you "think" you can clear it with a five iron, but you "know" you can with a six—go with the six. Good players take what the course gives them and, although you might not like it, if you have to give up some distance to ensure a better position for your golf ball then so be it.

Once you've evaluated your lie and the lip of the bunker, your last consideration is the length that you want to hit the shot. Obviously it's the lie and the lip that determine how far you can hit your ball. It might be 180 yards to the green, but with the high lip you must use an eight iron and unless you're Tiger Woods that means you're going to have to lay up.

The Set Up

You want to pick the ball cleanly off the sand, even hit the ball on the thin side to make sure you don't hit it fat. For stability, widen and open your stance (left foot back), keeping the majority of your weight on your left side. Play the ball in the middle of your stance and wedge your right foot against the sand and work your left foot into the sand just a bit. Stand a little farther from the ball than you normally would and reach for the ball by stretching your arms, which insures that you'll hit the ball a little thin. Grip down on the club about an inch, which shortens the shaft and also allows you to make a more controlled swing.

Think Ugly

We have a saying—"thin to win"—and it applies to your full swing and especially to fairway bunkers. You can play surprisingly good golf catching the ball a little thin, but if you hit it fat, you're history. If you do catch the ball slightly thin, it may look a little ugly but the result is usually good. Golf isn't a beauty pageant, but if it was, there is nothing more ugly than leaving the ball in the bunker. (Note that we said "slightly" thin—that's a lot different from topping the ball, an error that's as bad as the fat shot.)

To make "thin to win" a reality, cut down your backswing to three quarters for control. Your body turns, but there is very little weight transfer. By minimizing weight transfer, you guard against slipping or sinking into the sand at the top of your swing—a sure way to hit the ball fat.

Pitching

A pitch shot around the green, where the ball flies high and doesn't roll very far, is very much like a miniature version of your full swing. Since height is what you want, choose your most lofted club, your sandwedge, for your pitch shots. Here's a question you might win a few bets knowing the answer to: "What is the heaviest club in the bag?" Most people would say the driver or maybe even the three iron. The answer, however, is your sandwedge and that's another reason to use it for those pitches out of the rough, because it cuts through deep or wiry rough found around most greens.

The Three Basics of Pitching

To become a good pitcher of the ball there are three basic rules that, with practice, will help you get the ball consistently close to the hole.

Basic One: Aim then Align

At address, make sure your clubface aims at your target, because if you make a good swing, the ball goes in the direction the clubface is looking at impact. Now aiming the clubface correctly is about as basic as it gets, but you might be surprised as to how many junior golfers have trouble doing this. You'll be fine if you simply follow your pre-shot routine as laid out in chapter four

Aim the clubface at the target.

where you take care of your aim first with your clubface and then arrange your body in your set up without moving your clubface. To repeat, it's aim then align.

Basic Two: Butt in the Middle

No matter how long your pitch shot is, always line up the butt end of the club with the center of your body. Not only does this position maintain proper loft on the clubface, but it gives you a simple goal while you swing—keep the butt in the center of the body. Poor pitchers push their hands ahead of the ball at address which effectively decreases the loft of the club and they can't hit the high, soft pitch. Then during their swing, they pick the club up with no body

Butt of the club in the middle.

turn at all and chop down on the ball, a move than often causes fat shots. Shoving your hands ahead of the ball is also a good way to shank it, because it reduces the amount of hitting area you have to work with on the clubface, making contact dangerously close to the heel of your club.

Basic Three: The Same on Both Sides

To understand this basic of pitching, picture a clock and imagine that you're swinging your left arm to its numbers. If you swing back to nine o'clock you swing through to three o'clock. If you swing back until your left arm points to seven, then swing through till your left arm points at five. So the length of your backswing matches the length of your follow through. It won't take many pitches before your brain learns a very important lesson—when you contact the ball your club slows down a bit and through practice, you'll teach yourself how much your club needs to accelerate to account for it, so you'll have the same length swing on both sides of the ball. And although you won't have to think about it, the concept of acceleration transfers nicely to your full swing because you never want to be decelerating into the ball.

Swing the same on both sides.

Watch the great pitchers of the ball like Tiger Woods, David Duval and Justin Leonard and you'll see a beautiful, even pace to their motion back and through—it's called tempo. If your backswing is long and your follow through short, you'll have to slow the club down during your return swing or you'll hit the pitch too far. With this kind of deceleration of the club, you'll tend to hit the ground behind the ball. With a short backswing and an accelerated downswing into a long follow through, you'll tend to hit the ball too hard, or worse, hit the middle of the ball producing a long, low running shot—just the opposite of the high, soft shot you planned for. So maintaining an even length swing is contingent upon your ability to maintain your tempo and, when you do, you'll contact the ball cleanly and with no unpleasant surprises.

Distance Control

There is no rule on how far the pitch should fly because it depends on how strong a player you are; let's say that for an 11-year-old beginner, a long pitch might be 20 yards while a low-handicap 14 year old, it might be 60 yards. The point is that the terms long, medium and short are in relation to you rather than an objective standard. The key is to be able to create the right length of shot you need (short, medium and long) by making three simple adjustments to your set up.

Three Simple Adjustments

The distance you hit each shot is determined by three adjustments to your address position: the length of the club (how much you grip down on it); the width of your stance; and how open your stance is. The shorter the shot the closer your feet are to one another and the more your stance is open. Any time you use a narrow stance with your front foot drawn back in an open position, your swing becomes shorter and this shortens the distance your ball flies. You can also shorten the distance of your pitch shot by gripping down on the handle of your club, automatically creating a shorter swing arc and therefore less distance.

So here's the progression: a narrow, extremely open stance with the club gripped down, produces a very short shot. The longer the shot, the more you widen your stance, grip up on the handle toward the butt end, and make your stance more square.

Controlling the Height of Your Shot

How high the ball flies is controlled by three factors: the force of the blow to the ball; ball position; and your clubface position at impact (the more open it is the higher the ball flight). Opening your clubface increases the loft and bounce of the club, producing high trajectories. Closing your clubface has the opposite effect. How hard you hit the ball is determined solely by the length of your swing and you should make no attempt to create distance through manipulation of your hands and arms. The longer your swing, the faster your clubhead moves at impact which increases the height of your shot.

The farther forward (toward your left foot) you position the ball in your stance, the higher and softer the shot will fly; conversely the farther back you position the ball, the lower and more rolling the shot will be. So to hit a high,

Impact comes at the center line of the body.

soft shot you must position the ball forward in your stance or more toward the target. To hit normal shots the ball is positioned in the center of your stance, and to produce low, running shots, you move the ball back in your stance.

Say you hit your sandwedge 60 yards with your full swing. When you have a 30-yard shot you'll reduce the distance the ball travels in this way. First, shorten the length of your club by gripping down about one inch. The shorter the shaft, the shorter your swing arc and the less distance you'll generate. Next, narrow your stance slightly and then drop your left foot back so that your left toe is even with the ball of your right foot. From this position, the length of your backswing shortens because you can't turn as much and you'll have to swing shorter because, with the narrow stance, you'll lose your balance with a long swing. For a medium-length pitch, grip down to the middle of the grip, progressively narrow your stance, and open your stance by dropping your left foot back until your toes are even with the arch of your right foot.

For very short pitches, say ten yards or less, your hands are as low as possible on the grip, with your feet only a few inches apart and your left toe even with your right heel.

Pitching is like an underhand throw.

Pitching is Like an Underhand Throwing Motion

You can toss a ball with no problem so you should be able to hit good pitch shots because it's almost the same. To toss a ball a very short way, you would face your target with a narrow stance and your motion is upper body oriented, mostly an arm swing. For a short-distance pitch, you've learned that your stance is narrow and open and the length of your swing back and through is short. As you need to throw the ball farther, you'll naturally widen your stance to accommodate the longer arm swing and you make the same adjustment for pitching—the longer the shot, the wider the stance and the longer the arm swing.

Length of Arm Swing

Here is a guideline that will help you regulate the distance. For a short pitch, your hands never rise above waist high, for a medium-length pitch they swing up to the middle of your chest and for the long pitch they swing to about shoulder high. But remember, swing your arms as you would in your full swing, never lift your arms to these positions. As we shall see below, if you do it correctly, your hands and arms stay much lower than your clubhead because your clubhead is elevated above your shoulders by the setting (cocking) of your wrists. This gives you the clubhead height you need to get the ball up in the air, but keeps your arms and hands under control so they can accelerate smoothly through the ball.

Body Rotation

You should allow your body rotation to dictate the amount of swing that is produced, with your hands finishing at the same height as they were at the top of your swing. This way, the length of your swing will always match the length of the shot—short swing for a short shot, long swing for a long shot. Thus your backswing and follow through are a mirror image of each other and are controlled by the amount of body rotation as follows.

For all but the longest pitch shots, you should keep your weight on the left side of your body. This doesn't mean that you stand with a frozen body and just swing your arms up and down. For pitch shots you don't need any weight transfer from one side to the other and there's no time to do it in such a short swing. But do be sure to let your body rotate around your left hip axis as you swing the club. For long pitches you'll have a good deal of rotation, for medium distances you'll have some and for short ones, there will be very little body rotation during the backswing. The short shot is primarily an arm swing to waist high, but when the shot is longer your shoulders are included and as the shot continues to increase in length the final power source, the hips, become the focal point of your swing. For the full-swing pitch shot a weight shift from hip to hip takes place as your hands swing to shoulder height because, as we have said, the long pitch is a miniature golf swing.

Right elbow and wrists hinge simultaneously.

Right Elbow Fold

The triangle formed by your shoulders and arms remains intact until about waist high with the butt of your club pointing at your navel. There is no wrist cock until the weight of your swinging clubhead creates a natural hinging of your wrists. Only when your right elbow begins to fold, do

The Role of the Legs

Good pitchers of the ball have minimal leg action during the backswing while their upper body creates the length and leverage necessary for the shot. During the forward swing, however, there's a good deal of leg action with the right knee moving aggressively to the target. This "quiet-then-active" sequence is often reversed by the poor pitcher of the ball so that the lower body (hips and legs) are very active on the backswing but dead during the forward swing, leaving the hands and arms to over-manipulate the club.

your wrists hinge and the more folding and hinging that take place, the higher the ball flies.

Pitching Summary

The key to your upper body action is that while your hands and arms stay low, your clubhead is elevated above your shoulders by the setting (cocking) of your wrists. This gives you a position where the clubhead is high enough to loft the ball in the air, but your arms and hands are under control because they haven't moved very far from where they were at address.

For all your pitch shots from this range, your weight stays on your left leg as you swing the club. But as we warned above, don't just stand there on your left foot and swing your arms up and down as if you were chopping wood. Take care to rotate around your left hip axis as you swing the club.

You can always tell if a golfer is a poor one because his lower body (legs) is very active on the backswing, but dead during the forward swing leaving the hands and arms to over-manipulate the club. To be a good pitcher, however, do just the opposite—use minimal leg action during the backswing while your upper body creates the length and wrist cock necessary for the shot. During the forward swing, however, there's a good deal of leg action with the right knee moving aggressively towards the target.

So your hips and upper body turn the club away from the ball, but it's your lower body that controls the clubface during the downswing. A common mistake is to abruptly stop the arms at impact in an attempt to put a "hit" on the ball. When this happens, your left wrist collapses sending the clubhead past your hands in a flipping action that makes controlling the distance, and sometimes even the direction, of your shot almost impossible. You can avoid being a "flipper" by keeping your arms moving well into your follow through and to do this effectively you must keep your left hip rotating as you swing through the ball with no change of pace or speed—in other words you don't need to add or subtract any force, you simply "hit it with your turn" as we say. This ensures that you keep hitting down and through the ball with no unwanted bursts of power.

The Five Musts of Pitching

TIPS

1. The weight starts, stays and finishes in the left hip joint—there is no weight shift as there is for full swing, but...

2. There is a hip turn as in a full shot, only not as much.

3. There is very little leg action going back—the legs are quiet, but the arms are active—what turns is the hips and chest. This reverses in the downswing where the legs are active and the arms are passive. In the correctly executed pitch shot, the hands and arms feel "dead".

4. The club swings along the body line and the wrists cock the clubhead upward producing a low-hands-high clubhead.

5. You finish with the club shaft parallel to your body line as measured by your foot line, because there was no rotation of the forearms through impact. Note the back of the left hand faces the sky as does the clubface, indicating that the clubface has been kept open for softness.

Learning Programs for Juniors

Introduction

The main reason we wrote this book was because we felt there was a need for juniors to have a comprehensive guide for playing the game of golf. If you go into a large book store and go to the sports section, you will notice that somewhere between Football and Hockey is the Golf section. There you will find 30-plus books on golf, everything from *How to Cure Your Slice* to *Playing Golf After 70*. But, there are relatively few books written on Junior Golf. In *Play Golf For Juniors* you have learned how to swing, chip, putt and how to practice and you've learned a little about the rules, etiquette and how the game is played.

Now we take the next step in getting you onto the golf course. The best thing you can do at this point is to become involved in an organized group instruction program. The focus of this chapter is to clue you in on how you can become involved in these kinds of programs. If chosen correctly, these programs are invaluable as they not only provide quality instruction in all phases of the game, but also get you on the course to use what you have learned.

The Program at PGA National

Here at PGA National we have a quality program involving hundreds of junior golfers. Director of Golf at PGA National, John Gardner, explains our purpose this way: "Each year hundreds of children participate in one of the most comprehensive programs offered to junior golfers anywhere. Personal instruction, tournament programs, seminars on golf etiquette and the rules are all provided to participants in the program. We applaud the efforts of the staff of the Academy of Golf and PGA National Golf Club for their efforts on behalf of junior golf."

Gardner goes on to describe the nuts and bolts of the program. "In terms of instruction, we offer a four-day junior golf camp with three days of instruction followed by the fourth day when a tournament is held to complete the program. The tournament is a scramble format where each player tees off and the foursome decides to take the best drive of the four. The other players pick up their balls and go to the spot where the best drive landed and hit their second shots from that point. This continues until someone on the team holes out. Each team must use a drive from every member of the team at least once, so everybody is included—it's a great format and the kids love it."

The following schedule is the one we use here at PGA National, but there are countless ways instructional programs are put together. More about them later.

This is a four-day camp that always starts on a Monday and this outline will give you an idea of what to expect from the program.

Monday:

Report to the designated practice area

7:30–8:15 a.m.	**Orientation to the game of golf**
8:30–9:15 a.m.	**Full Swing**
9:15–10:00 a.m.	**Pitching**
10:00–10:45 a.m.	**Chipping**
10:45–11:30 a.m.	**Putting**
11:30 a.m.–12:30 p.m.	*Lunch*

| 12:30–2:00 p.m. | Skill testing: Putting and Chipping |
| 2:00 p.m. | Starting times reserved on Champion golf course to play golf. |

Tuesday:

Report to practice area

7:45–8:15 a.m.	Registration
8:30–9:15 a.m.	Full Swing
9:15–10:00 a.m.	Pitching
10:00–10:45 a.m	Chipping
10:45–11:30 a.m.	Putting
11:30 a.m.–12:30 p.m.	*Lunch*
12:30–2:00 p.m.	Etiquette—Classroom
2:00 p.m.	Starting times reserved on Squire golf course to play golf

Wednesday:

Report to practice area

7:45–8:15 a.m.	Registration
8:30–9:15 a.m.	Full Swing
9:15–10:00 a.m.	Pitching
10:00–10:45 a.m.	Chipping
10:45–11:30 a.m.	Putting
11:30 a.m.–12:30 p.m.	*Lunch*
12:30–2:00 p.m.	Rules of the game—Classroom
2:00 p.m.	Starting times reserved on Squire golf course to play golf

Thursday:

Report to practice area—instruction on tournament rules

| 7:30–9:00 a.m. | Registration—Groupings will be posted Wednesday. Participants are to arrive at least 30 minutes prior to assigned starting times. |
| 8:04–9:32 a.m. | Opening Tournament: Four-Person Scramble |

The above is just a brief outline of the junior instructional program used here. In addition to this format there is a tournament series including the Junior Club Championship, Parent Junior Nine Hole Scramble, The One Club Tournament, The Pro-Junior Cayman Ball Tournament, The Four Person Scramble Tournament, and several more.

Junior Programs in General

Throughout the country in nearly every city or town there are golf courses and driving ranges that have junior instructional programs, so there's no shortage of places to learn the game. Junior Programs are part and parcel of nearly every golf facility and the reason is simple: juniors are the future of the game. If we want the game to survive we have to have a steady stream of new and well-educated players entering into it. Think of it like the college draft in football. The National Football League gets its new players from the colleges across the country. Junior programs are golf's college draft system so to speak and that means juniors are the lifeblood of the future.

There are more junior golf programs for children of all ages today than at any other time in the game's history, so it's not a matter of programs being available, but whether or not you're going to take advantage of them. An issue that is continually being addressed is access to golf courses for juniors so that they can actually play the game. Most private golf courses have off-peak times after school and on weekends set aside for juniors to play golf. At public golf courses, the issue for juniors often revolves around the management's policy concerning the use of golf carts. For example, if they have a mandatory cart policy, the junior player would either have to be accompanied by someone with a valid driver's license or walk the course, without an adult, in the late afternoon, often after 2:30 p.m. The minimum age to walk the course without being accompanied by an adult varies from club to club and depends on the type of insurance policy the courses carry.

There are Family Golf Centers springing up all across the country designed specifically to provide juniors with the same access to a golf course as the adults, but there is still a minimum age limit and, to avoid embarrassment, you should call to check with the facility to see what their policy is. Now this may sound a little complicated just to play a round of golf, but when you think about it, it's no different than any other organized sport. If you were to sign up for Little League or Soccer it would be the same thing. You would have some sort of registration, you would have get the proper equipment to play the game, you would have practice sessions, there would be rules, etiquette and some form of supervision. You would be given a schedule of when the practices and games are going to take place and so on. So golf is really just like any other sport in that regard.

And after all the formalities are taken care of, what's left is the fun of hitting a golf ball far into the distance toward the target or making a great putt and seeing the ball roll into the hole.

Why Golf Needs Good Junior Programs

Make no mistake about it, you the junior golfer are the hope and future of the game and you will make it a better game for all who play it. It's for these reasons that so much thought, energy, care and planning goes into the development of junior golf programs.

Those of us that are in golf as our chosen profession know that when people who play golf are products of junior golf programs, they are not only better golfers in terms of shooting good scores, but they are better for golf in every other aspect as well. We are now seeing the effects that junior golf programs have had on golfers who participated in these programs who are now adults. Players who were products of these programs are more respectful about such things as fixing their divots, ball marks on the greens, raking sand traps and the like. There is an increased sense of fair play, more honesty and a passion for playing by the rules. When players have been associated with a good junior golf program, respect for their opponents and fellow competitors is much more evident. Junior golf programs develop these qualities in kids and all of us who play the game are better for it.

And certainly one of the biggest threats to the game of golf is slow play, something that takes the fun out the game for everyone. But we are seeing that those who are junior program graduates play faster and better. The good news is that these traits developed in junior programs, tend to stay with you throughout your whole life, and isn't that what golf is—it's a fun game for your whole life.

Some Programs You Should Know About

The following are examples of programs available to juniors provided by the PGA Junior Golf Foundation.

PGA Junior Medallist Program: This program is a golf skills practice and recognition program to help youngsters improve their game. Juniors achieving certain standards in putting, chipping, pitching and driving can qualify for awards. The following is a quote from the PGA Junior Journal:

"A vast number of skills are required for anyone to become a proficient golfer. One look at the different leaders in each of the PGA Tour's statistical departments demonstrates that nobody plays a perfect game. A golfer can only become a stronger player by practicing the weakest part of their game. And juniors need to realize that a bad shot is not always as bad as they think."

The PGA Medallist Program tries to help junior players to develop their skills by breaking down the game of golf into six distinct categories, these are: putting; chipping; pitching; fairway irons; driving; and sand play.

"Throughout the program, professional instruction, individual practice and testing focus on these vital skills as well as sportsmanship and rules. Each skill is rated at three levels of achievement—bronze for beginners, silver for intermediate and gold for advanced. As junior golfers progress through each of these skills, they receive a series of awards. The value of the PGA Medallist Program is that it objectively determines the strength and weaknesses of a junior in each of the designated skills. One junior may be excellent in several skills, but may have trouble in other areas. Time is well spent providing instruction and assistance, so that each junior can pass all the skills to achieve the ranking he or she is striving for."

Other programs include **Clubs for Kids** which is a golf club recycling program whereby used clubs are donated to youngsters wishing to start playing golf.

PGA Junior Cadet Program: A new, modified caddie program to provide youngsters with golf training and playing opportunities on the course.

Computer Search

Do you own a computer or have access to one? The PGA has a web site—"http://www.pga.com"—address, that devotes a section with several links where juniors can browse through topics of interest. The section is called "Cool Kids" and the following examples are the types of things that you will find at this site.

Junior Tournaments: There are national junior golf tournaments held throughout the country sponsored by the PGA of America and others affording juniors the opportunity to compete at the national level. There are, of course, qualifying events at the local and regional levels prior to the national competitions. In this link on the main web page you will find all the information that you would need to participate. Things such as the concept and the purpose behind the tournament, the history of the tournament, registration forms so that you can enter on line, entry fees, the application process, rules, prizes and an explanation of the point system and exemptions. There is also a Frequently Asked Questions section that answers any other questions that you may have about participation.

Get Your Kid Started in Golf: This is the PGA of America's introductory golf program called "First Swing" which emphasizes the teaching of fundamentals of the golf swing for juniors. This program is probably the most widely used method in the country. Facilities in practically every city in the United States use this program or one very similar to it.

Take the Cool Kids Quiz: Another link on the PGA web page. Here you will find a quiz that will test your knowledge of golf and the topics change every week. For example, this week's topic tests your knowledge of golf terms. Take it and see how you do.

Send In Your Questions: This is Steve Jubb's link, he's the editor of *PGA Junior Journal*. Steve is ready to help you with a variety of questions you might have on getting started in golf ... from golf camps, school golf activities and programs to community programs, colleges and universities, tournaments, equipment, etc. Included here is an e-mail address for you to use for your questions.

Junior Style Rules: The rules of golf can be pretty tricky so here they have given you the rules in what they call "Junior Summary Form" which does state 28 of the 33 rules, in simple language.

Local Junior Golf Info: This link shows you how the PGA is divided up into sections across the United States and how to contact the one that is nearest to you, to receive information about various junior golf programs in your area. According to this link "the easiest way for junior golfers to get in touch with the proper PGA professionals is to contact the section office they're interested in. Boys and girls of all ages are participating in these programs so please don't wait, contact your local PGA section office and sign up today for a meaningful golf experience".

Junior Golf Etiquette: This page helps you to understand the ins and outs of etiquette, and a lot of people who play golf violate the rules of etiquette without even knowing they are doing it.

We hear different stories from the rangers at our golf complex, but the theme is the same: a violation is spotted and the offender is told about it and says, "Oh, I'm sorry, I didn't know," and, of course, that is exactly the problem—they didn't know! Fortunately, we don't often see these kinds of things happening with golfer's who are products of junior golf programs.

In closing this chapter we have made it clear that you're greatly valued as junior program participants and future adult golfers. With the information provided here you should understand that you can easily become involved in both learning and playing regardless of where you live, your economic situation or even if you have a disability. The American Disabilities Act has made it law that disabled people must have access to a golf course. So get out there and take advantage of the great opportunities that exist today for junior golfers, you won't believe how much fun you're going to have.

Tournaments

Well you've certainly come a long way if you're ready to play in tournaments. Tournamants are a big deal and adherence to the rules is more strict, but some juniors (and especially their parents) get all up tight about this kind of stuff. Our advice is to do the best you can and enjoy yourself and if you like the competition—keep competing. Hey, maybe you'll be the next Tiger Woods and when they interview you on national TV, you'll say you owe all your success to this book and then we'll be rich and then ... well let's get to it.

Winning and Losing

Before we begin, a brief word on winning and losing, because how you feel about yourself and your performance will have a lot to do with how you play. The concepts of winning and losing are too often thought to be interchangable with success and failure. They are not the same because you can be very successful in tournaments and still lose. Here's how you need to approach it: "I gave it my best shot and for whatever reason I didn't win, but giving it all my effort makes me a success." This is how champions think.

Note the difference between "not winning" and losing. Losing is a state of its own, a state where losers dwell: "not winning" is tied to "winning"—it's a state where both winners and non-winners live, the other side of the coin. In a golf tournament with 100 participants and one winner you don't have 99 losers. You have 99 players who did not win and that's a big distinction. The only way you become a loser is if you quit and don't try on every shot. Please don't take what we are saying, however, to mean that you should be happy with mediocrity. You should always do your best, whether it's tidying up your room, taking a history test or hitting a two iron on the 18th hole. Excellence is a habit—remember they didn't call him Alexander the Mediocre.

On the Two Basic Types of Competition

As we have said, all golfers are treated the same under the rules, showing that golf plays no favorites because at the end of the competition it's what you shot (medal play) or how many holes you win (match play) that counts. Most of your golf, at first, will just be golf, the game—hit the ball, find the ball and hit it again until it's in the hole. You're not playing against anyone and you're not even keeping score, just having fun. As you progress you may want to compete, so it's a good idea to learn the difference between medal play and match play—the two most popular tournament formats of the game.

In medal play competition you're playing against all the golfers who are playing and you record your score (how many strokes you took, plus penalties) for each hole. Your opponent is everyone that's playing and the lowest total score after everyone has finished is the winner. It's cumulative and the previous score carries forward to be added to the next hole score. Thus every stroke counts and because of the cumulative nature of stroke play the strategies are often different from match play where the winner is the one who has won the most holes. A hole in match play is won by recording fewer strokes then your opponent and the hole victory/loss carries forward, but the strokes that provided the win or loss do not. Holes where you both have the same number of strokes are tied (halved). Halved holes are not simply ties however, but play an important role in determining the strategy and the final winner. You could reach the

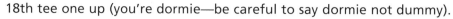

18th tee one up (you're dormie—be careful to say dormie not dummy).

In stroke play competition the size of the field means that you won't be playing head up with most of your opponents and you may have to play under different conditions than those who played when the wind was down or it was raining. In match play you can see what your opponent is doing and adjust accordingly—and you both play the same course at the same time. It's face to face, mano a mano or womano a womano.

Keeping Your Game Ready for Competition

Regardless of whether you're playing match or medal, you have to keep your game tournament ready. How do the tour players do it? They know how to practice: they have a pre-shot routine that's both physicial and mental; and they keep themselves physically fit. Let's take a look at each of these in detail.

Practice

One way, of course, to keep your game sharp is to play in a lot of tournaments and the other is to practice correctly. As you might expect, experts are very good at practicing—they know exactly what kind of practice is correct given the situation. Below are described the kinds of practice that will help you to keep your game ready for competition.

Just hitting balls for the sheer joy of it can be really fun and you should do this as often as you can. This is the purest form of practice with no rules, and for no other purpose but enjoyment. Still, keep in mind that there are four types of practice: 1. warm up; 2. fundamental building; 3. targeting; and 4. practice as you play. It's a good idea when you're practicing seriously to keep each area separate and in the next section you'll learn why that is important.

Warm Up

All practice sessions begin with a warm up, to prevent injury. A good warm up includes three stages: stretching that works all the major muscle groups; practice swings without a ball where your club never stops moving; and hitting very short shots that give you the feeling of solid

Always warm up to start.

contact. Once you've done this you're ready for either practcie or play.

There is nothing worse than hitting two inches behind the ball on your first warm up swing and the solution is simple—tee all the balls while you warm up. There is something about the feel of hitting it on the sweet spot that lets you know you're going to play well, so make solid contact your major goal during the warm up.

Note: The best way to get ready to play on the course regardless of whether it's a tournament or just a regular round, is to do your stretching routine and then program yourself for solid contact by hitting a few shots with a teed up seven iron. You shouldn't turn your warm up into a swing overhaul session. The worst thing you can do five minutes before tee time is to be searching for a swing.

Fundamental Building

To play better and to enjoy the game more, you've got to keep your swing in shape by working on your fundamentals (grip, stance, posture, takeaway, etc) and the place to do that is on the practice tee, under the direction of a qualified set of eyes. But be careful, because fundamental practice sessions can turn into boredom unless you change the task about every 15 minutes. If for example, you're hitting a six iron have them switch to a nine iron and then switch to a driver and then back to a six iron. Or start hitting pitch shots and then switch back to the driver or switch to a game in which you hit low shots. The point is to prevent boredom, because once you are bored your mind goes on scan and productive learning stops.

Note: It's important that when you're working on something like the grip or the takeaway you shouldn't judge how well you did it by the ball flight, but soley on how well you performed the fundamental that you're practicing.

"Doesn't Every Shot Start With A Target?"

The third part of your practice session is focused on the target—where you want the ball to end up. When you use this kind of practice, work on hitting shots to target. And don't forget to go through their entire pre-shot routine—that way it will be more like the real thing. Switch targets with every shot just like you do when you play—one on the left side of the range, one in the middle and a target on the right side. If you begin to hit the ball poorly, abandon target practice and return to fundamental practice. Make this a game where you have to announce when you're switching to another practice type. Ask yourself from time to time "which practice type am I using?" Doing it this way, it won't take long for you to realize that there is a big difference in practice types.

Practice Like You Play

Show the kids how they can actually play a round of golf right there on the practice range, using their imagination to lay out the course in their mind, then going through their pre-shot routine and hitting the ball to the target. Play the game together, desciving the shot you're about to make. It might be a left to right par four or a straight-away 540-yard par five with water in the driving area on the right side. Practicing like this is a great way to prepare for the course and it's fun.

Pre-Shot Routine

Obviously there is more to playing tournament golf than having a good swing. A study done at Wilfrid Laurier University in Canada showed that while most of the emphasis in junior instruction is placed on swing mechanics, psychological skills, such as mental preparation and concentration play, an important role in performance. The study measured nine factors that influenced a junior's handicap and found that the most important was the way a junior prepared mentally for the shot. The lower the handicap the more the junior: 1. visualized where the ball would finish; 2. planned how best to play the entire hole before teeing off; 3. worked out specifically where to place each shot as part of their mental rehearsal.

The data showed that junior golfers were less able than adults to separate negative emotions and concentration. When they got upset, they allowed it to break their concentration and the juniors who were taught to handle the mental control, showed the least interferance and the lowest handicaps. One way to make sure you're thinking correctly while you play is to develop your pre-shot routine.

A Good Routine is Both Physical and Mental

First, take care of direction by aiming your clubface and aligning your body correctly at address. Once this is done, forget about the direction of your golf shot and let your golf swing produce the correct distance your shot needs to travel. Design your routine so that you fix the direction first, then the distance—and always in that sequence. Stand behind your ball and plan your shot. Make sure your practice swing is a true rehearsal of the up-coming shot by taking it in the direction of the target and at the same speed as the swing you are about to make. Once you've pictured the shot in your mind and have made a practice swing, take a deep breath to relax.

The pre-shot routine is not just a procedure you go through before you swing, it is an important part of the swing itself and no expert player is without one. Your brain loves routines and a good routine calms you down, because you're doing the same things in the same order for every

Pre-shot routine.

Always aim and align before taking your stance.

shot. It's all too easy to get excited and to speed up your swing when you're actually playing on the golf course. But if you have a good routine it protects you against the tendency to disrupt your rhythm under stress by either speeding up or taking too much time. It's like going into a protective bubble when you develop a solid routine, an insulator that

The full set up.

Check your grip.

Now you're ready to pull the trigger.

shields you from outside distractions like noise and people moving around while you're trying to hit your ball. And once you start your routine it's like an avalanche that takes you directly to impact, so you can pull the trigger with confidence every time.

Billy Casper, one of the greatest golfers of all time also had one of the best pre-shot routines of all time. He did exactly the same thing every time and if something distrubed him while he was in his bubble, he'd stop and start all over again. He even went so far as to put the club he'd selected for the shot back in the bag, even if he was knew he was going to use that club for the shot. This way he asssured himself that he would repeat the exact steps every time.

What's in a Routine

Always stand behind the ball to make your plan—and get into the habit of having a plan for each shot. A golfer without a plan is like going on a journey without a final destination—you're liable to end up anywhere and so is your ball. So approach each shot from directly behind the ball, looking down your intended target line to your target. It's very helpful to pick out two spots, one just in front of your ball on the line to the target (we'll call it an intermediate target) and the other where you want your ball to land. And be as specific as you can about where you want your ball to fininsh. So here's what you do: draw an imaginary line back from your target, through your intermediate target (it could be a divot, old tee or some other mark), and back to the ball—now tell your brain that you want to hit your ball along this line to the target.

Now it's time to move to the ball and aim your clubface along the imaginary line you have drawn to your target. To do this, step into your address position with your right foot leading the way. Before you bring your left foot into position, sole your clubface behind the ball, so that it points at the target. Then, keeping your clubhead in its exact position, bring your left foot into position so that your body is perpendicular to your clubface. You have now locked in your direction.

And by aiming your clubface and aligning your body correctly at address, you've taken care of the direction part of the equation. Once this is done, forget about the direction of your golf shot and let your golf swing produce the correct distance your shot needs to travel. Design your routine so that you fix the direction first, then the distance—and always in that sequence.

Now step into your address position with your right foot leading the way. Before you bring your left foot into position, sole your clubface behind the ball, so that it points at the target. Then, keeping your clubhead in its exact position, bring your left foot into position so that your body is perpendicular to your clubface. You have now locked in your direction. From this position, take one look at the target to finalize your distance calculation by rotating your head without lifting it, waggle and pull the trigger, allowing the speed of your swing to produce the correct distance. This procedure takes only about 30-45 seconds and if you make it a habit, your priorities will be correct for every shot—direction through address, distance through swing speed.

Keep Yourself Injury Free

Another thing the Tour pros do to keep their game tournament ready is to protect themselves against injury. Here is a little know fact—kids can get hurt playing golf. Even though, as a junior golfer, you might seem super-

The wrong way to pick up your golf bag.

flexible, a surprizing number of kids have golf-related back problems. Research at the Chichester Institute in Chichester, England reported that about 14 per cent of the junior golfers in the study had golf-related back problems serious enough to require medical attention, while 41 per cent of the sample reported golf-related pain after playing or practicing.

Granted, it's hard to get kids to do things that will prevent back

The correct way to tee up your ball—with your knees flexed.

problems. For the most part they feel bullet proof, as we all did when we were young, but to keep them injury free it's worth the effort. The research showed two ways to prevent injury: warm up before you practice or play and be careful how you bend and lift. Here is what you need to know to keep yourself healthy.

1. All practice sessions, even the short game, should begin with a warm up, the purpose of which is to get blood flowing into your golf muscles. A warm up routine also puts you in the mood for what is to come, allowing you to put aside your non-golf concerns so that your mind will be free to focus on your practice session. You should personalize your warm-up routine depending on your body profile (strength, flexibility etc), but in general it should include three stages: a stretching program that works all the major muscle groups; a continuous series of dry-run swings without a ball, where your club never stops moving; and a ball-striking progression, starting with partial swings, that build slowly over ten balls, to full swings.

2. In golf you do a lot of bending. You pick up your ball, retrieve the ball from the hole, tee your ball up, pick up your tee after you hit. The second way to protect your back is to be careful how you bend down.

3. Be careful of your back and avoid heavy lifting. When you bend over, even to do something as benign as brushing your teeth, keep your knees flexed and your back straight rather than hunching. Lifting your clubs from the trunk of your car is a real back breaker, so make sure to keep your knees flexed and rest them against the bumper when you lift.

On the course: When you're teeing a ball or picking it out of the hole, flex your knees and squat rather than doing any stiff-legged bending. If you carry your bag, be especially careful picking your bag off the ground. Even if you have one of those modern carry bags with the legs, you can get your spine into some bad angles, so always flex your knees and try to have your spine straight when you lift.

Tournaments—Where You Can Tee It Up

There are numerous local junior tournaments in your area and all you have to do is call the state golf association to get a list. On the national level, the most comprehensive and best-run program comes from the PGA and it's called the PGA Junior Series.

About the PGA Program

The Purpose of the PGA Junior Series is to provide junior golfers with affordable and competitive playing opportunities in professionally supervized events organized by the PGA Tournament Corporation, a subsidiary of the PGA of America. The Series (12 stroke play events) provides increased national exposure for boys and girls. The 144-player field will consist of approximately 50 per cent from the host state and 50 per cent from outside the host state. Each Series event is open to boys and girls who are at least 13 years of age and who are under 18 years of age on the final day of any event they enter. The four age group divisions consist of Boys/Girls: 13–14 and 15–17. Competitors may enter as many or as few events as they wish. The PGA also encourages all junior golfers to continue to compete in your local PGA junior golf events. There have been 22 events conducted over the past two years in 14 states with total participation from 45 states and four countries. The average participation is 15 states per event. The entry fee is $40 for a 36-hole competition and $60 for a 54-hole completion.

The Maxfli Jr. Championship is played on The PGA National Champion Course, the same course as the PGA Seniors' Championship. The Maxfli PGA Junior Championship's nearly 100-player field is composed of champions from the PGA of America's 41 sections and selected winners of national championships conducted throughout the year.

† Past participants in the championship who have all gone on to a successful career on the PGA and LPGA Tours include: Danielle Ammaccapane, Billy Andrade, Brandie Burton, Heather Farr, Rick Fehr, Jim Gallagher Jr., Vicki Goetze, Justin Leonard, Michelle McGann, Billy Mayfair, Phil Mickelson, Dottie Mochrie, Scott Verplank, Willie Wood and Tiger Woods.

Glossary

Lever:

An arrangement of your body and club that multiplies your power: left arm 90 degrees to the shaft is one example.

Blending:

Your arms do the up and down, and your body does the around and they don't get into each other's business.

The Ball As Teacher:

Once you've learned your swing, you make adjustments to it based on ball flight. The ball is your teacher when you're adjusting your swing.

Aim and Alignment:

You aim the clubface and align your body.

"Mark your ball":

To place an object such as a small coin behind your ball to identify its original position once the ball is removed.

Toe:

The end of the clubface opposite the heel.

Loft:

The angle of the clubface as measured from the leading edge to the top line of the club when the club is soled flush to the ground.

Anatomical Snuff Box:

Term for the depression just above the joint of the thumb.

3 Grip Types:

Strong—left hand on top of shaft with the shaft between the left thumb and one target thumb.

Weak— left hand to left of shaft thumb down the left side of the handle.

*Neutral—*left thumb on top of shaft with the back of the left hand to the target.

Lob Wedge:

More lofted than the average sandwedge with about 60 degrees of loft. It is used to hit high shots that produce minimal roll. Leave it out of your bag until you're a low-handicap player.

Square:

Clubface pointing at target, body aligned parallel left of target.

Open:

Clubface points to right of target; body line points left of target.

Closed:

Clubface points to left of target; body line points to right of target.

Foot Flare:

Amount foot is turned out from perpendicular or 90 degrees.

Takeaway:

First part of the swing that ends with a wrist cock.

Setting the Angle:

Cocking the wrists to create a lever.

Fore:

A warning signal called out by golfers to warn others that they may be in danger of being hit.

Coil:

A ratio such as 2:1 where the shoulders turn more than the hips.

Achieve then Leave:

Know what you want to accomplish during your practice session, and when you do stop practicing.

Birdie:

Holing out your ball in one swing less than par.

Bogey/Double Bogey:

Holing out your ball in one/two swing(s) more than par.

Par:

The score an expert is expected to make.

Lag Putt:

A putt that assures that the next putt is easy. A long putt that would be difficult to hole out should be lagged close to the hole for an easy two putt.

Pull:

The golf ball travels on a straight line, but to the left of the target.

Choke Down:

The action of placing your hands farther down the grip of your club so that there is an inch or two between the butt end of your club and the top of your hand.

Dog Leg:

Golf hole that is curved or angled from right to left or left to right. (Resembling the shape of a dog's hind leg.)

Eagle:

Two strokes under par for a particular hole. Most commonly achieved on a Par 5 where a long hitter may be able to reach the green in two shots, rather than the allotted three, and one putt for a score of three.

Rough:

Areas on the golf course, usually adjacent to the fairways and surrounding the green, which are comprised of thicker, longer grass than is found in the fairway.

Sky Ball:

Similar to a pop-up in baseball. It sometimes leaves scratches on the top edge of the driver called "idiot marks".

Tee:

The teeing ground itself is the tee.

Slice:

The golf ball curves severely from left to right.

Push:

The golf ball travels on a straight line, but to the right of the target.

Fat:

Term used to describe a mis-hit shot where the club comes into contact with the ground before striking the ball itself.

Honor:

The right to tee off first due to having the lowest score on the previous hole or awarded on the first tee on the basis by lot.

Lie:

The way in which the sole of your golf club rests on the ground. It can lie toe up and therefore be too upright, it can lie with the heel up and therefore be too flat, or it can lie with the sole flush to the ground and the toe slightly up which is the standard.

Fringe, Apron or Collar:

Area immediately surrounding the putting surface, often cut at fairway height.

Heel:

The portion of the clubface located toward the hosel or neck of the club.

Getting the Angle:

Cocking the wrists creating a lever.

Index

Note: Page numbers in italics indicate that a topic is referred to in an illustration, but not in the text, on that page.

address 76, 80, 134
  pitching 111, 112, 113
aim 55–7, 111, 131, 134
arms, and chipping 100–101
  and pitching 115, 116, 117
  and splash shot 107
  strength 72–3
  and swing 60–63, 65, 71, 75, 79, 81, 85
back problems 135–6
balance 15, 80, 83
ball position 55, 88, 100, 105, 107, 108, 114
balls, identifying 29
behavior on the course 23–4, 25, 26, 31–3, 125
body rotation, pitching 116
bounce 20–21, 103–4, 108, 113
bunkers 21, 29, 32
  explosion shot 107–9
  fairway 109–11
  lies in 103
  splash shot 103–7
carts 33, 121
chipping, ball position 100
  compared with pitching 95–6
  drills 101–2
  flight-to-roll ratio 96–8
  similarity to putting 98–9, 100–102
  stance 99–100
clubface, at impact 16, 40, 56, 66, 72, 101
  in explosion shot 108, 109
  in pitching 111, 113–14
  in splash shot 103, 104, 107

squaring 55–6, 76, 79, 82, 85
clubhead, in pitching 115, 117
  speed of 14, 70, 78, 80, 81, 114
clubs 12, 16, 19
  and effect on swing 13, 15–16
  lie angle 17–18
  recycling 123
  shafts 14, 15–16
  throwing 78
  weight 13–14
Clubs for Kids 123
coil 61, 62, 71, 72, 81, 83, 84
  importance of 74
  maximizing 63, 85
competitions, practice for 128–30
  strategies in 127–8
competitiveness 37, 38
concentration 130–31
contact, and swing 66–7
Cool Kids Quiz 124
courses 22
  access for juniors 121
development, physical 38–9, 59
direction 56, 131, 134
  in putting 93
distance, and loft 18–19
  in pitching 113
  in pre-shot routine 131, 134
  in putting 92, 93
divots 18, 24, *27*, 32–3
downswing 65–7, 69, 71, 72, 75, 78, 81
drills 70–71, 101–2
driver 18, *53*, 54, 55, 84
drops 27–9, 30–31
elbows, in pitching 116–17

and swing 61–2, 76, 77, 79, 82
etiquette, explained 125
    see also behavior on the course
explosion shot 107–9
failure 35–6, 37, 126–7
fairway bunkers 109–11
fairways 21
Family Golf Centers 121
feet, position 54–5, 71, 80, 99–100, 114, 134
finish position 67–9, 81, 83, 102
"First Swing" program 124
flight-to-roll ratio 96–8
follow through 67–9, 75, 80, 109, 112
girls, adjustments for 71–3
greens 20, 98
    moving balls on 27
grip, checking *133*
    importance of 40
    learning 46–9, 73
    pressure 50
    for putting 89
    types of 49–50
grips 16
hands, and putting 87–8, 89
    see also grip
hazards 29–31
hips, and aim 56
    and pitching 116, 117
    and swing 64, 66, 74–5, 80, 81, 85
hole-in-one 23
impediments 27, 29
injuries 134–6
irons, and ball position 55, 84
    and fairway bunkers 109–10
    flight-to-roll ratio 96–8
    grip for chipping 99
    and loft/distance 18–19
    in practice 129
    and set up/stance *53*, 54
junior programs *see* learning programs
knees, in pitching 116, 117
    and posture 51, 54

and swing 77, 79, 85
learning, and enjoyment 37
    phases of 40–41, 43
    set up 45–6
    swing 46
learning programs 118–19
    at PGA National Golf Club 119–20
    benefits of 121–2
    and skills 123
lie angle 17–18
lies 27
    in bunkers 103, 109–10
    improving 25, 27
    unplayable 27, 28
loft 18, *19*, 21, 104, 112, 113–14
losing 126–7
lost ball 26
match play 127
Maxfli PGA Jr. Championship 137
medal play 127
motivation 35–7
mulligans 24
order of play 26–7
out of bounds 31
par 22–3
parent/child relationships 35–6, *39*, 40–41, 43
penalties 28, 29, *30*, 31, 104, 127
PGA Junior Cadet Program 123
PGA Junior Journal 124–5
PGA Junior Medallist Program 123
PGA Junior Series 137
PGA National Golf Club, learning program 119–20
PGA Tournament Corporation 137
PGA web site 124–5
picking up 24–5
pitching, distance control 113, 115
    height control 113–14, 117
    with sandwedge 111
    swing 112–13, 114, 115–17
planning 91–2, 98, 130, 133–4
posture 15, 45, 50–52, 76, 77, 79, 80, 83
practice 128–30, 136

pre-shot routine 57, 130–34
preparation, mental 130–31
putters 18, 19
    choice of 20, 91
putting 86–7
    aggressive approach 91–2
    and distance 92, 93, 95
    drills 93, *94*, 95
    pendulum stroke 88–91, *94*, 95
    stance 90
relief 28, *30*, 31
respect 122
rules, summarized 26–31, 125
Rules of Golf 24, 31
sandwedge 18, 19, 97, 103, 108
    pitching with 111, 114
scorecards 23
self-esteem 37
shafts 14, *15*
shoulders, and aim 57
    and chipping 100, 102
    and explosion shot 109
    and pitching 116
    and splash shot 107
    and swing 63–4, 78, 79, 82, 85
skills, and learning programs 123
    mastery of 38
    psychological 130–31
slow play 24–6
soleing the club 28, 29, 91, 95, 134
spin 56
spine 52, 64, 67, 79, 82
splash shot 103–7
stance 52, 54
    in fairway bunkers 110
    for pitching 113, 114, 115
    for putting 90
    for splash shot 104–5, *106*, 107

strategies, in competitions 127–8
success 36–7, 126–7
swing, affected by clubs 13, 15–16
    and club variety 59–60
    and contact 66–7
    downswing 65–7, 69, 71, 72, 75, 78, 81
    eliminating errors 73–4
    explosion shot 107, 108–9
    in fairway bunkers 110–11
    fundamental practice 129, 130
    junior teaching program 124
    learning 41, 46, 58–9
    models of 35, 74–85
    overswing 72
    pitching 112–13, 114, 115–17
    in pre-shot routine 131–2
    and set up 44–5
    takeaway 60–62, *64*, 70, 77
    top of 63, 71, 76, 81, 82, 85
target practice 130
tees 25, 28, 129
tempo 112–13
tournaments, for juniors 124, 137
    in learning programs 119, 120
warming up 128–9, 136
wedges 20–21, 54, 97
    see also sandwedge
weight of clubs 13–14
winning 126–7
woods 19, 20, 54, 55
Woods, Earl 34–6, 43
Woods, Tiger 27, 34–6
wrists, and chipping 99, 101–2
    and grip 49, 50
    and pitching 115, 116–17
    and putting 95
    and swing 61, 62–3, 76, 79, 80

Picture Acknowledgments

The publishers would like to thank the following sources for their kind permission to reproduce the pictures in this book:
Allsport (U.K.) Ltd/Craig Jones 34